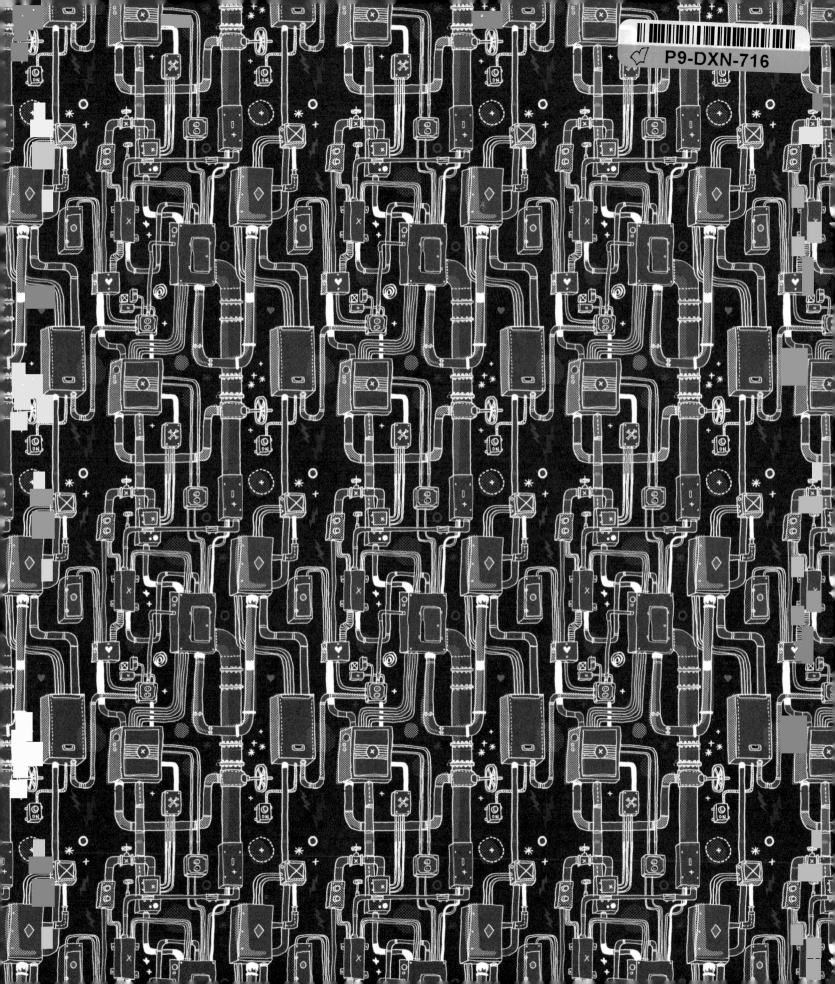

underworld

EXPLORING THE SECRET WORLD BENEATH YOUR FEET

This edition published by Kids Can Press in 2014
First published in Australia by Weldon Owen Limited in 2012
© 2012 Weldon Owen Limited

Kids Can Press acknowledges the financial support of the Government of Ontario, through the Ontario Media Development Corporation's Ontario Book Initiative.

Jane Price started her career writing fiction for teenagers and is the co-author of the *Lonely Planet Not-For-Parents Travel Book*. Jane lives in Sydney, Australia, with her husband, three excitable children and a large brown woolly dog.

James Gulliver Hancock grew up in Sydney, Australia, and has worked in illustration, animation and design all around the world. His other books include *All the Buildings in New York* and *What on Earth*. James currently works out of his studios in Brooklyn, New York, and Sydney, Australia.

Published in Canada by
Kids Can Press Ltd.
25 Dockside Drive
Toronto, ON M5A 0B5

Published in the U.S. by
Kids Can Press Ltd.
2250 Military Road
Tonawanda, NY 14150

www.kidscanpress.com

Creative Director Sue Burk
Editor Emma Hutchison
Designer Emilia Toia
Kids Can Press edition edited by Caitlin Drake Smith

This book is smyth sewn casebound.
Manufactured in Malaysia, in 10/2013, by Tien Wah Press (Pte) Ltd.

CM 14 0 9 8 7 6 5 4 3 2 1

Library and Archives Canada Cataloguing in Publication

Price, Jane (Jane Paula Wynn), author
    Underworld : exploring the secret world beneath your feet / written by Jane Price ; illustrated by James Gulliver Hancock.

Includes index.
ISBN 978-1-894786-89-8 (bound)

1. Underground construction — Juvenile literature. 2. Underground areas — Juvenile literature. 3. Underground ecology — Juvenile literature. 4. Earth (Planet) — Internal structure — Juvenile literature. I. Hancock, James Gulliver, illustrator II. Title.

TA712.P75 2014   j624.1'9   C2013-905298-4

Kids Can Press is a Corus™ Entertainment company

underworld

EXPLORING THE SECRET WORLD BENEATH YOUR FEET

WRITTEN BY
JANE PRICE

ILLUSTRATED BY
JAMES GULLIVER
HANCOCK

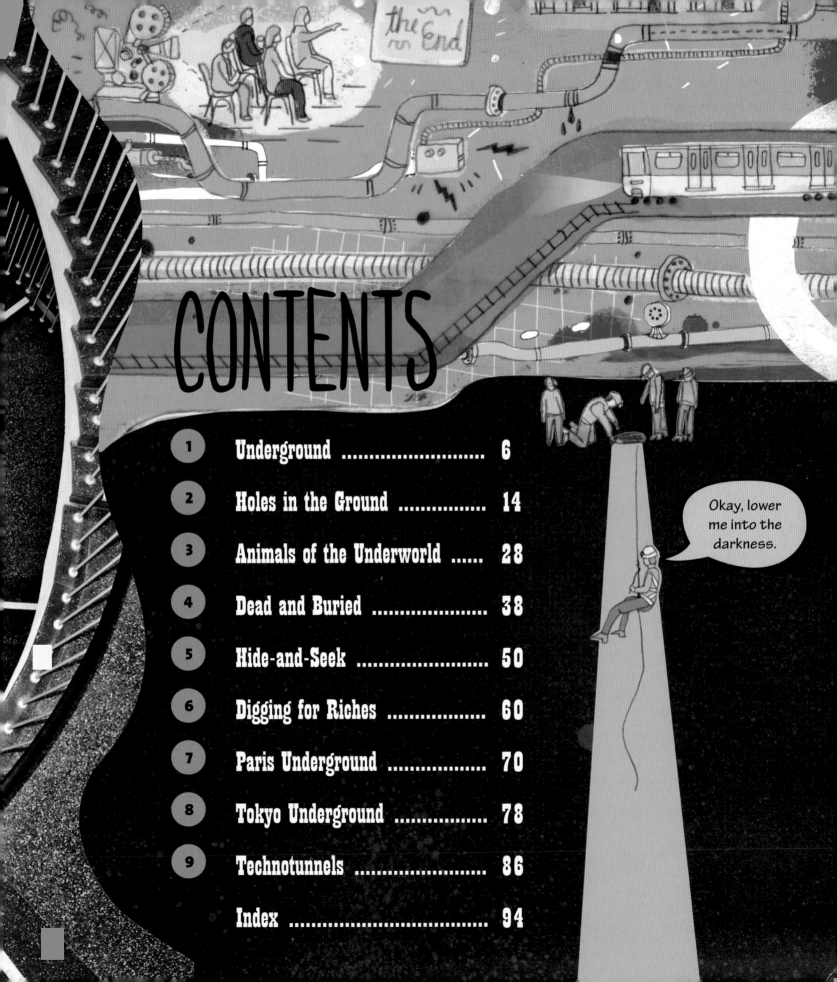

CONTENTS

Okay, lower me into the darkness.

CHAPTER 1

Underground
Earth's Crust and Below

Fold mountains

Landslide

Ocean

Two plates crash against each other.

Fossils in Earth's crust

Oceanic crust

The seafloor cracks as the plates move: earthquake!

Two plates move apart.

Earth's mantle

Boiling magma (liquid rock)

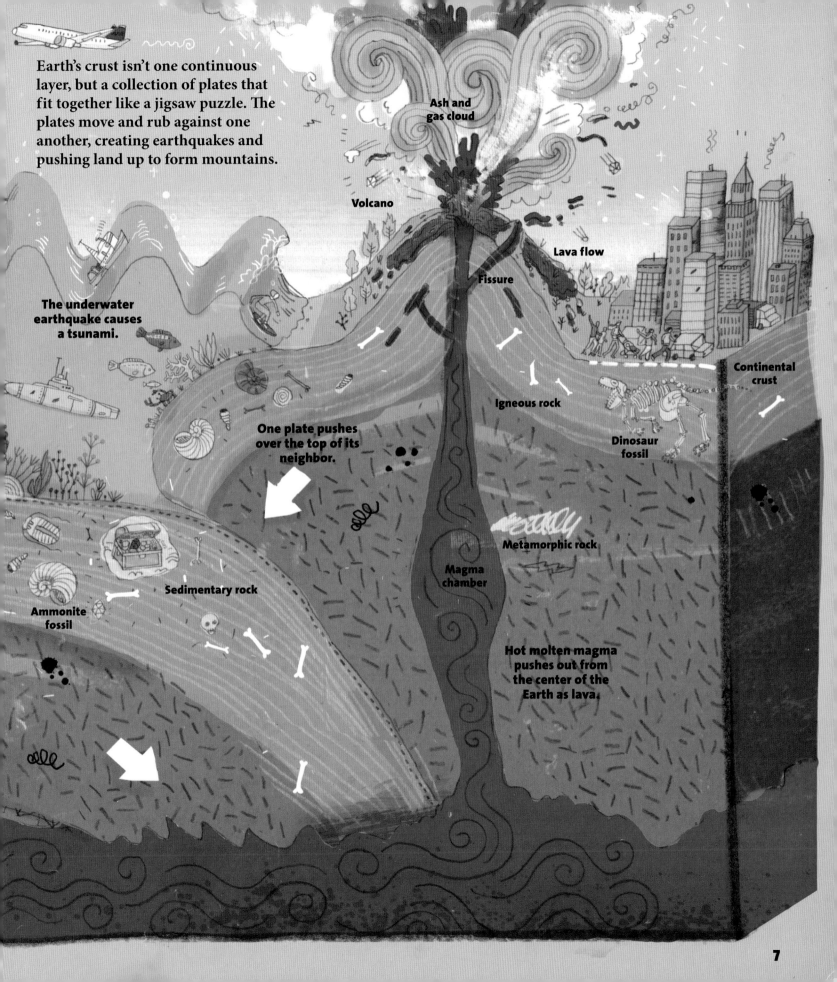

Earth's crust isn't one continuous layer, but a collection of plates that fit together like a jigsaw puzzle. The plates move and rub against one another, creating earthquakes and pushing land up to form mountains.

Ash and gas cloud

Volcano

Lava flow

Fissure

The underwater earthquake causes a tsunami.

Continental crust

Igneous rock

Dinosaur fossil

One plate pushes over the top of its neighbor.

Metamorphic rock

Magma chamber

Sedimentary rock

Ammonite fossil

Hot molten magma pushes out from the center of the Earth as lava.

7

JOURNEY TO THE CENTER OF THE EARTH

If you could dig a tunnel to the middle of our planet, you'd have a long, hot journey through four different layers. Below the thin crust where we live is the mantle of hot liquid rock and gas. Beneath that is the outer core of boiling molten iron and nickel. At the very center of the planet is the inner core. Scientists believe this is a solid ball of iron and nickel about 2500 km (1500 mi.) in diameter — like an enormous metal bowling ball that's as hot as the sun.

ROCK AROUND THE CLOCK

Earth is made entirely of minerals, and different minerals combine to make rock. All rocks can be split into three different personality types (that's if rocks had personalities, of course).

2 **Igneous** rocks are the fiery kind. They are formed when magma, hot liquid rock under Earth's crust, reaches the surface and solidifies as it cools down. Granite and pumice are good examples.

3 Never trust **metamorphic** rocks — they're changeable characters! They used to be sedimentary or igneous rocks, but heat and pressure in Earth's crust have changed them into something else. Marble is sedimentary limestone transformed by heat. You can often see bands of different minerals in these rocks.

1 Three-quarters of the rocks found on Earth's surface are **sedimentary**. They are formed from tiny particles of eroded rock — the particles crush together over time to make a new rock.

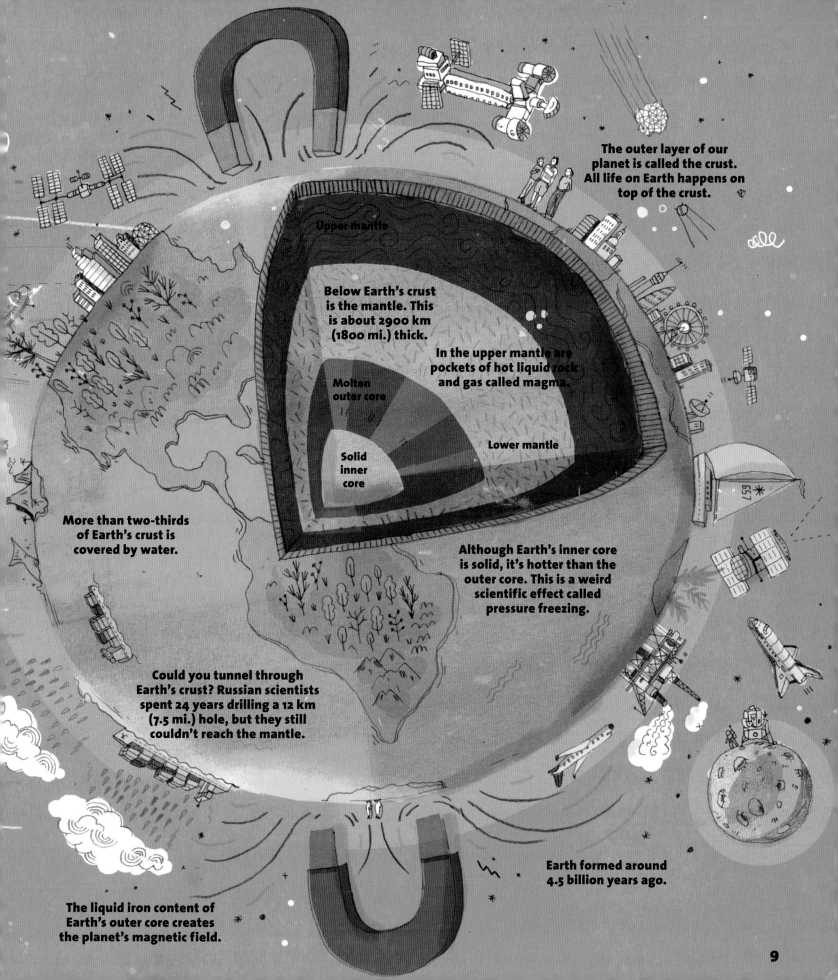

The outer layer of our planet is called the crust. All life on Earth happens on top of the crust.

Upper mantle

Below Earth's crust is the mantle. This is about 2900 km (1800 mi.) thick.

In the upper mantle are pockets of hot liquid rock and gas called magma.

Molten outer core

Lower mantle

Solid inner core

More than two-thirds of Earth's crust is covered by water.

Although Earth's inner core is solid, it's hotter than the outer core. This is a weird scientific effect called pressure freezing.

Could you tunnel through Earth's crust? Russian scientists spent 24 years drilling a 12 km (7.5 mi.) hole, but they still couldn't reach the mantle.

Earth formed around 4.5 billion years ago.

The liquid iron content of Earth's outer core creates the planet's magnetic field.

KNOW YOUR VOLCANO

Not all volcanoes are perfect pointy cone mountains. Volcanoes come in many shapes, including:

 1 Cinder cone: Lava erupts into the air, cools into pumice and falls back down to make a cone-shaped pile. So this volcano grows each time it erupts.

 2 Shield: Scientists think this volcano looks like a warrior's shield. It is wide with gentle slopes made by lava flowing down it in all directions.

WHAT'S A VOLCANO?

■ *There are more than 1500 active volcanoes on Earth. Eruptions can be "explosive," shooting rock and lava high into the air, or "effusive," squeezing slow-moving lava from fissures.*

A volcano is like an enormous bursting pimple on Earth's skin. Boiling magma in Earth's mantle builds up pressure and forces its way out through cracks (fissures) in the crust. Magma that has erupted is called lava. It can shoot into the air to harden into pumice rock or flow down a side of a volcano, destroying everything in its path.

■ *The eruption of Krakatoa in Indonesia in May 1883 was the loudest explosion in recorded history. It was heard 4800 km (3000 mi.) away.*

LOST POMPEII

The explosive eruption of Mount Vesuvius in 79 CE destroyed the busy Roman city of Pompeii in a single day. Citizens were killed by falling pumice and toxic gas and buried for 1700 years.

3 **Stratovolcano:** This is the king of the volcano world. Its gently sloping sides grow steeper toward the top and its eruptions are explosive, shooting lava, rock and gas high into the air.

An ash cloud can shoot 45 km (28 mi.) into the atmosphere.

Airborne pumice

Lava flow

Fissure

Earth's crust

Earth's mantle

Magma chamber

■ *Volcanoes are named for Vulcan, blacksmith of the Roman gods, who made lots of heat and noise — and perhaps erupted occasionally!*

■ *Even Pompeii's pets were stopped in their tracks.*

CAUGHT IN TIME

The remains of Pompeii's people vanished over time, leaving perfect molds in the rock. Archaeologists were able to make plaster copies of them. They also uncovered ovens with bread still inside and perfect wall frescoes.

DINOSAUR DETECTIVES

> I'm going to keep moving so I don't turn to stone.

Underground is a treasure trove for paleontologists (dinosaur experts). Strange stone bones found in the ground puzzled scientists until dinosaurs were recognized as a separate group of reptiles in the early 19th century. After that, digging for fossils, discovering new dinosaurs and choosing their names became the new craze. Dinosaur fossils have been found on every continent on Earth except Antarctica. Scientists have deduced that dinosaurs appeared 230 million years ago and disappeared 65 million years ago.

FUZZY FOSSILS

We think of fossils as animals or plants buried underground and turned to stone, but woolly mammoths frozen in ice and insects trapped in amber are also classified as fossils.

HOW ARE FOSSILS MADE?

Most fossils are created in watery graves. A plant or animal's remains are covered by mud and sediment and gradually harden into rock.

1 A dead dinosaur lies on the bed of a lake. Its flesh rots or is eaten by water creatures, leaving only its bones.

2 Over time the bones are covered by layers of mud and silt, preventing them from being washed away.

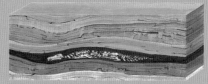

3 The silt turns to rock and the dinosaur's remains are replaced by minerals, leaving a perfect fossil copy.

4 Millions of years later, movements of Earth's plates bring the fossil closer to the surface.

Dracorex hogwartsia *is a fossilized dinosaur found in 2003 and named after Harry Potter's school.*

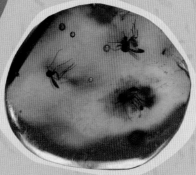

These unlucky flies landed on sticky tree resin 20 million years ago. The resin fossilized to amber and now the flies are trapped forever.

Ammonites are the fossils of ancient cephalopods (such as squid and octopi) that lived in Earth's oceans more than 200 million years ago. They died out at the same time as dinosaurs.

GIANT MYSTERIES

People dug up dinosaur fossils for thousands of years without knowing what they were. The Chinese thought they were dragon bones and in 1676 a British professor decided that one large fossil must be a giant's thigh bone.

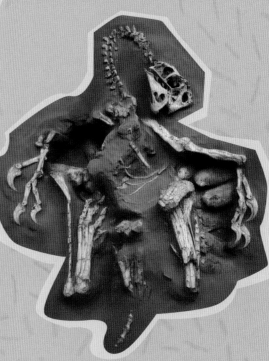

This oviraptor mom was covered by a Gobi Desert sandstorm 80 million years ago. She turned to stone protecting her eggs.

How did you know I was so good-looking?

Paleontologists can recreate an entire dinosaur skeleton from just one tiny fossil bone — like solving an enormous jigsaw puzzle.

13

Stream

Sinking stream

Cave city

Stalactites

Stalagmites

Crystal cave

Shaft

Wet cave

Limestone

holes in the ground

Crystals and Cave Cities

The surface of Earth's crust isn't all smooth rock — it's riddled with cracks and holes called caves. Many caves contain amazing formations called speleothems. Others give us clues about our own history.

Dry cave

Prehistoric cave art

Limestone cave

Underwater cave

HOW CAVES ARE MADE

A cave can be as small as a broom closet or hundreds of kilometers/miles long. Caves form when decaying plants in the soil release carbon dioxide. Rainwater passing through the soil picks up the carbon dioxide and continues its trickling journey down through the rock. The acidic water dissolves minerals in the rock, making cracks, tunnels and caverns. This doesn't happen quickly, of course: caves form over thousands, or even millions, of years.

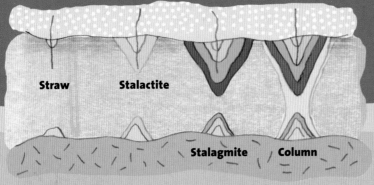

Straw   **Stalactite**

Stalagmite   **Column**

MEETING IN THE MIDDLE

Stalactites form on the roof of a cave and grow downward. They are often formed around thin, hollow tubes of calcite called "straws." **Stalagmites** grow up from the cave floor and are formed from the drippings of overhead stalactites. The two can join (very, very slowly) to form a column.

DRIP, DRIP

That constant dripping you hear in a cave is the rock roof being dissolved by acid water. Calcite in the water hardens to form straws, stalactites and stalagmites.

MIND YOUR HEAD!

If the cave ceiling dissolves so much that it becomes very thin, it may collapse. The cave then becomes a sinkhole.

Speleothems, such as the stalactites and stalagmites above, are cave formations created by minerals in dripping water.

A lava cave, left, is made when hot volcanic lava cools and hardens on the outside, but is still runny inside, like a soft-boiled egg. The molten lava slowly drains out, leaving a hollow tunnel of volcanic rock.

A glacier cave, right, is made by ice warming and melting into water. The water runs through the middle of the glacier, leaving a tunnel behind.

FROSTBITE OR BURNS?

Iceland's Kverkfjöll mountains are active volcanoes. Here, molten lava can bubble up through glaciers and a hot stream runs through a 30 km (19 mi.) ice cave.

BLUE BEAUTY

The entrance to Italy's Blue Grotto is large enough for one rowing boat. Roman emperor Tiberius used the grotto as his private swimming pool 2000 years ago.

CENOTE SINKHOLES

Cenotes are underwater sinkholes. The two main sinkholes of Cenote Dos Ojos in Mexico lead to one of the longest underwater cave systems in the world.

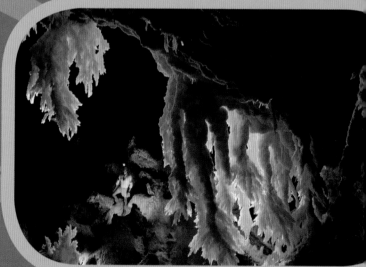

BOY WONDER

Jim White was just 16 years old when he discovered New Mexico's Carlsbad Caverns. He used a kerosene lantern and a ball of string to explore them.

AMAZING CAVES

Imagine you've squeezed through a hole in the ground and found yourself in a maze of pitch-dark tunnels. How would you measure or map them? Speleologists (cave scientists) used to map the underworld by pacing out distances with torches, but now they take it easy and use computers!

HOLD ON TIGHT!

Oman's Majlis al Jinn is one of the world's largest caverns. The ceiling is as high as a 36-story tower, and the only way into the cave is to be lowered on a rope.

Hey, guys, you can pull me up now. ... Guys?

SINKING CIRCLES

The largest of the Sarisariñama sinkholes in remote Venezuela is 300 m (1000 ft.) wide and deep. Rare plants and animals live at the bottom.

WORLD RECORD HOLDERS

1 **Mammoth monster:** The world's longest cave system is the aptly named Mammoth Cave in Kentucky. It's 644 km (400 mi.) long and parts of it are 100 million years old.

2 **Going down ... again:** Krubera Cave, in the country of Georgia, is the world's deepest cave, and it keeps getting deeper. The first explorers measured it at 1710 m (5610 ft.) in 2001. In 2004 it measured 2000 m (6562 ft.), and by 2007 it measured 2191 m (7188 ft.). It's not supersizing — explorers just keep finding new tunnels.

3 **Big show-off:** The world's biggest cave chamber is Sarawak Chamber, Malaysia, which was found in 1981 by three English cavers. It's 700 m (2300 ft.) long, 400 m (1312 ft.) wide and 70 m (230 ft.) deep — which makes it three times the size of Carlsbad Caverns' Big Room, the previous record holder.

4 **Keep swimming — it's a long way:** The world's longest underwater cave system is the Sistema Ox Bel Ha in Mexico, at 243 km (151 mi.). Mexico has all three of the world's longest underwater caves.

THE CAVE OF CRYSTALS

In April 2000, two Mexican silver-miners were working 300 m (1000 ft.) underground, digging a new tunnel. They noticed a hole in the limestone and, being curious, squeezed through. It was like climbing into a giant's jewelry box: a huge, steamy cavern full of crystals the size of tree trunks. These enormous slabs of sparkling selenite are the largest crystals ever found. Scientists estimate they are 600 000 years old and supersized because of the heat and water that filled the cave before the mining company drained it.

A nearby magma chamber makes the air so hot that anyone who enters the cave must wear a protective suit and breathing mask. Without them, a human's lungs can sizzle within 15 minutes.

A BAD IDEA

When the cave was discovered, some miners got carried away with their enthusiasm for huge crystals and carried the crystals home. The mining company put a heavy steel door on the cave to lock it up. One miner sneaked in through a narrow hole with plastic bags full of cold air to breathe while he looted crystals. His air bag idea didn't work very well — he was found dead the next day.

CRYSTAL CLEAR

The word "crystal" comes from the Greek kryos, meaning "icy cold." The Greeks thought that clear rock crystal was ice frozen so solid it could never melt. Earth is made from rock, rock is made from minerals and minerals are made up of crystals. Crystals form when liquid inside Earth cools and hardens. The temperature and pressure affect how the atoms in the mineral arrange themselves layer by layer. The most prized crystals grow with parallel edges and faces.

GET TO WORK!

There's no rest for a busy crystal. Tiny chips of silicon crystal are fitted in computers and bank cards. Quartz crystal, which can vibrate more than 30 000 times a second, is used in watches. And for thousands of years people have believed that crystal energy can cure illnesses.

CAVE CITY

If you were being chased and needed to hide, where would you go? Underground, of course! The underground cities carved into the soft volcanic rock of Cappadocia in Turkey were used by early Christians to hide from Roman troops. (They were built much earlier — the Christians just renovated before moving in.) Above ground are strange pointy rock towers known as "fairy chimneys," which were also hollowed out to make homes. When the Christians heard the hoofbeats of their enemies' horses, they hurried downstairs to hide.

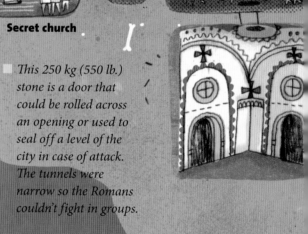

Home

Birdhouse

Dining room

Secret church

GOING DOWN

Cappadocia has 200 underground cities: the largest has 11 stories, all going down. More than 30 000 people lived there. The caves had air vents, wells, food stores, homes, wineries, oil presses, stables, churches, dining rooms and a school. Long, dark tunnels led off to other underground cities in the distance.

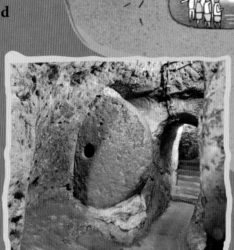

■ *This 250 kg (550 lb.) stone is a door that could be rolled across an opening or used to seal off a level of the city in case of attack. The tunnels were narrow so the Romans couldn't fight in groups.*

■ *Most of the underground passages were lit with torches, but some had light wells to bring sunlight to the lower rooms.*

■ *The Christians were persecuted for their religion, so they built more than 600 secret churches under the ground in Cappadocia. Take that, Romans!*

■ *Thousands of birdhouses have been found here. The Cappadocians certainly loved their pigeons — as tasty roast dinners, and for their droppings, which made the crops grow.*

23

UNDERGROUND ART GALLERY

In September 1940, four teenage boys looking for their dog discovered the Lascaux cave under the French town of Montignac. They returned with flashlights and shone light on an art gallery from 17 000 years ago. Paleolithic humans made these paintings over many hundreds of years.

GRAND DESIGNS?

Archaeologists aren't sure why Paleolithic humans decorated this cave, but they know they weren't just trying to make a designer home. The paintings are in narrow, dark tunnels, where the artists would've had to crawl with small, spoon-shaped stone torches of burning animal fat in their mouths.

1 **The Hall of the Bulls,** near the entrance, has bright white walls that make it a perfect canvas. One of the bulls painted here is 5.2 m (17 ft.) long — the largest cave art animal ever found.

The Hall of the Bulls contains paintings of horses and stags, as well as bulls.

TOO MANY ART-LOVERS

The artists used red and yellow ochre and black manganese from the ground around the cave to make their drawings. In 1948, electric lights were fitted inside the cave and 100 000 people per year started coming to look. Quickly, the colors faded and algae grew on the walls. The caves were closed in 1963, but a perfect replica was built on the same hill for visitors. It took ten years to paint.

There are more than 2000 figures painted in the cave. More than half of the animal figures are horses. After horses come stags, aurochs (large wild oxen, which have been extinct for 500 years), ibexes and bison.

The stags below appear to be swimming. Only their heads and antlers are painted, bobbing above an area of dark rock that must have looked like water to the artist.

2 **The Painted Gallery** features the Ceiling of Red Cows, the Great Black Bull, the Falling Cow and the Upside-Down Horse.

3 **The Passageway** links the Hall of the Bulls to the Shaft of the Dead Man. Archaeologists explored the shaft first — they thought it would lead to a burial tomb. It didn't.

4 **The Chamber of the Felines** features the only bears and cats depicted in the cave. These carnivores hide in the deepest, darkest parts of the cave — just like they do in real life.

5 **The Wounded Man** is the only human figure in the cave, but he's not a very good painting — he's just a stick figure compared to the carefully painted animals.

The Wounded Man is falling as a bison charges. This is the only painting that seems to tell a story. Below the man a bird perches on a stick.

The man's face is drawn to look like a bird's face, and birds are sometimes used to signify death. Creepy!

GATEWAYS TO HELL

What did ancient civilizations make of volcanic eruptions, clouds of burning ash or dark tunnels leading into the ground? Many of them believed that caves, volcano craters and other holes led straight down to hell. With all that hot magma bubbling under the surface, who could really blame them? The Mayans, Greeks and Romans all had caves they believed to be gateways to hell. Enter if you dare!

■ *Souls of the damned journey to hell through the crater of Iceland's Hekla volcano, according to cheery Icelandic folktales. Bedtime story, anyone?*

■ *Dante's Inferno is a famous poem about hell. It tells the story of Dante, who gets lost in a dark wood and travels down through nine layers of hell to reach the center of the world.*

The Mayans thought their underworld gods lived in the Actun Tunichil Muknal caves in Belize, and threw human sacrifices down to them. One of the 100-year-old skeletons explorers found inside had been completely calcified, making it sparkle when light is shone on it. They nicknamed it "The Crystal Maiden."

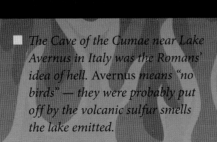

All these stairs are hell on my knees.

The Cave of the Cumae near Lake Avernus in Italy was the Romans' idea of hell. Avernus *means* "no birds" — they were probably put off by the volcanic sulfur smells the lake emitted.

Austria's Eisriesenwelt caves were found by excited explorers in 1879. Actually, no ... the terrified locals knew the caves were there all along, but didn't dare go in because they believed they were a gateway to hell.

CHAPTER 3

animals of the underworld

Hide-and-Seek

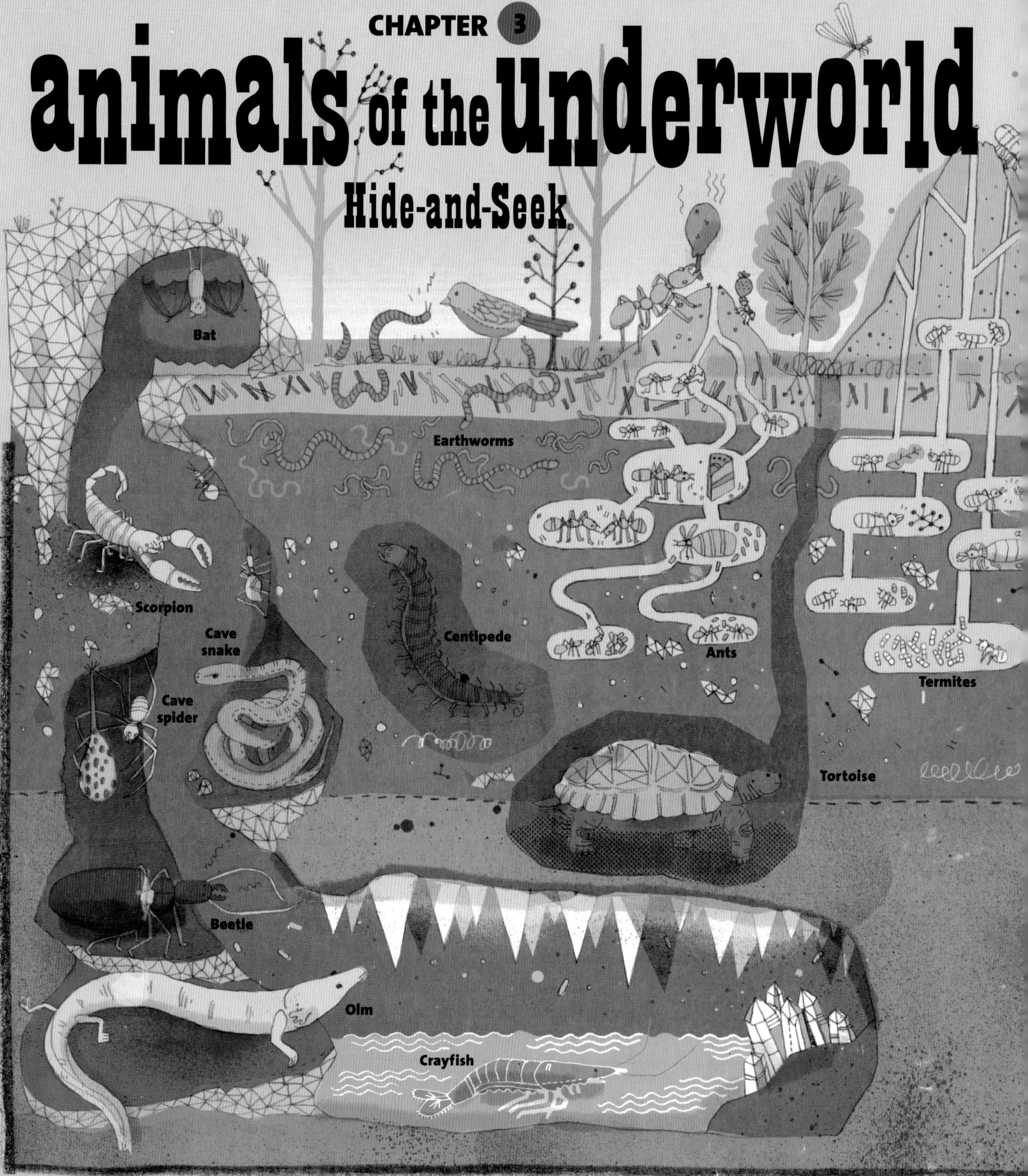
Bat
Earthworms
Scorpion
Cave snake
Centipede
Ants
Cave spider
Termites
Tortoise
Beetle
Olm
Crayfish

Squirrel

Fox

Rabbit

Garter snake

Cicada

Wombat

Armadillo

Dormouse

Prairie dog

Meerkat

Animals have made their homes underground for millions of years to keep themselves warm or cool and out of sight of predators. Some dig their own burrows, while others live in caves.

Naked mole rat

A LIFETIME OF DARKNESS

Many creatures live underground, but some live more underground than others. Trogloxenes shelter in the spooky dark entrance to a cave, but will happily venture out into the world above to look for food. The best-known trogloxenes are bats, but others include spiders, beetles and fish.

Deeper in the cave live troglophiles, who love their cave but could survive on Earth's surface if they had to. Their name comes from the Greek *trogle*, meaning "cave," and *phile*, meaning "to like."

In the deepest, darkest part of the cave live the troglobites. These species have adapted to cave life and cannot survive outside. They often have no pigment (color) in their bodies and are almost transparent. Many have no eyes (who needs eyes when there's no light?), but have grown long antennae or legs to feel their way in the dark.

Out of every ten caves on Earth, nine are left unexplored because they don't have an entrance we can see from the surface. Scientists have named 7700 species of troglobites, but they know there are many more underground. Even in well-explored caves, troglobites are experts at hiding — hide-and-seek is much easier when it's dark and you're transparent!

WHAT'S FOR DINNER?

Because there's no plant life deep in the cave, the troglobite's usual diet is the dead bodies of other troglobites or delicious guano (bat poo).

The blind scorpion rarely ventures into the light. It has no eyes — its enormous pincers make up for that.

Adult cave spiders hate light, so they settle deep in the cave. But when baby spiders hatch from the egg sac, they are attracted by light and leave the cave to spread the species. Clever!

When the albino cave crayfish stands still, it becomes invisible to predators.

IN THE ZONE

Scientists divide the ecosystem of a cave into four zones:

1 **The entrance zone** is where Earth's surface and underground environments meet. Huge colonies of bats often make their home in the shadowy entrance zone.

The cave-dwelling beauty rat snake can twist and turn to catch bats hanging from the cave roof.

That snake's a beauty ... now get flying!

2 **The twilight zone** is below the entrance zone. There is less sunlight here, but a few plants are still able to grow. This is the special place where troglophiles feel happiest.

Some species of blind cave beetles have been found in only one or two caves in the world. Anophthalmus hitleri was discovered by a German collector in 1933 and named for Adolf Hitler.

3 **The transition zone** is almost entirely dark, but there is still a hint of what's happening on Earth's surface. Breezes and air movements can be felt and loud noises can still be heard from the world above.

The olm was the first troglobite to be discovered, in 1689. Heavy rain washed millions of olms out of caves in eastern Europe. Scared villagers thought they were baby dragons.

4 **The deep cave zone** is completely and permanently dark. The air is always damp and still and no sounds can be heard from the world outside. This is where troglobites scuttle and glide in the darkness.

BATWORLD

Bats are trogloxenes and live in the cave entrance zone, where the sunlit surface of Earth meets the dark underworld. Even trogloxenes can get confused — some colonies of bats live under bridges that they think are caves. Bats spend their days hanging from the cave roof and come out at dusk to hunt for insects. Only vampire bats can run along the ground to take flight; other bats have to use their front legs to climb up somewhere high and then fall into the air from there.

WEIRD WEATHER

Some bat colonies are so large that when they emerge from their cave at dusk, they show up on weather radars and confuse weather forecasters.

BLOODSUCKERS

Vampire bats are the only creatures to live on a diet of blood — the blood of sleeping animals, birds and even humans! They can drink half their weight in blood and get so full they have to push themselves off the ground with their special long thumbs. Vampire bats don't suck blood Dracula-style — they bite their prey and then lap up the blood. They're not so scary when you find out they're only the length of a thumb!

BAT FACTS

The world's largest bat colony has 40 million bats. But even in a crowd this big, a mother bat can use smell and sound to find her own baby where she left it.

JUST HANGING AROUND?

For a bat, roosting on the cave ceiling is the safest place to be. Who's going to attack it there? The tendons in a bat's claws grip automatically when it relaxes its body. The bat's weight keeps its claws closed so it can hang without using any energy.

There's nothing I love more than hanging around!

HEAR THE ECHO?

Bats find their way in the dark by echolocation. The bat makes a high-pitched sound and listens for the echo that comes back. It uses the echo to map out nearby objects and avoid bumping into them. There's one big problem with bat echolocation — it doesn't work well in the rain.

SWIMMING IN THE SKY?

Bats might fly like birds, but their wings are more like human arms with long fingers at the ends. Their wings are thin layers of skin stretched between their "fingers" and their bodies and legs. Bats don't flap their wings like birds: they move more like humans swimming the breaststroke.

DARK DENS AND BEASTLY BURROWS

Many animals dig burrows to sleep in during the day, then emerge at dusk to hunt for food. Paleontologists have even found dinosaur remains in burrows that were dug 95 million years ago. The dinosaurs were the size of cats and were cold and scared — their land was frozen and they were hunted by meat-eating dinosaurs 50 times their size. You can imagine why hiding underground seemed like a good idea.

Some burrows are simply long, twisting tunnels ending in snug chambers where animals can curl up and go to sleep in safety.

Birds usually build nests in trees, but Magellanic penguins build theirs in burrows, which protect the birds from the elements, but not from itchy fleas.

The wombats of Australia hide themselves so well underground that European settlers didn't even notice them until ten years after they'd arrived.

Don't wake me until spring.

When winter weather sets in and food is scarce, many animals hibernate to save energy. This isn't just like taking a long sleep — their breathing and heart rates slow down and their body temperature drops.

Now, where did I hide the rest of those nuts?

Female polar bears dig maternity burrows when they're ready to give birth. The mother and her cubs stay in the burrow for four months or until the babies are big enough to venture out.

Some hibernating animals, such as squirrels and chipmunks, store food in their dens and wake every couple of weeks to take some deep breaths and have a snack. Others eat a lot in late summer to build up body fat, and then don't eat again until spring.

Snakes are cold-blooded and can't keep themselves warm in winter. They don't undergo the same physical changes as animals that hibernate — instead they shelter in holes and become dormant so they appear to be dead.

THE WEIRD WORLD OF THE NAKED MOLE RAT

Imagine a bustling animal city beneath your feet. While a burrow can be a cozy home for one or two creatures, some animals dig an enormous maze of tunnels and chambers and live together in a colony. The funny-looking naked mole rat is perfectly adapted to live with its family and friends in a dark, but well-organized, underground city.

Naked mole rats feed on underground tubers, such as potatoes. They nibble away only part of the tuber so that it keeps growing — a never-ending meal.

Sausage-shaped body, 7 cm (3 in.) long, perfect for tunnel life

No fur

Tiny eyes that can see only light and dark

Who are you calling a sausage with teeth?

Long whiskery hairs to feel the way

Short, sturdy legs

Powerful walrus-like teeth used for digging

Pink, saggy, naked skin that does not feel pain

BUSY DIGGERS

The tunnels of a mole rat city can stretch up to 5 km (3 mi.) under the dry grasslands of east Africa.

Some naked mole rats venture above ground to find plants or seeds.

This dark underground world provides cool shelter from the hot African sun.

Each naked mole rat has a job for life: digging tunnels, finding food, looking after the queen or protecting the colony from snakes.

The naked mole rat lives longer than any other rodent on Earth — its record is 28 years.

Up to 300 naked mole rats live in one colony.

A JOB FIT FOR A QUEEN

The boss of the colony is the queen. She has three male mates and is the only female who can give birth. The queen nurses her pups for one month, then hands them over to nanny workers, who feed them poo until they are big enough to eat plants.

dead and buried
Into the Ground You Go!

Stone Age humans were the first to bury friends and family in the ground. Perhaps this is when they started to think about life after death? Or maybe they just thought it wasn't a good idea to leave bodies lying around.

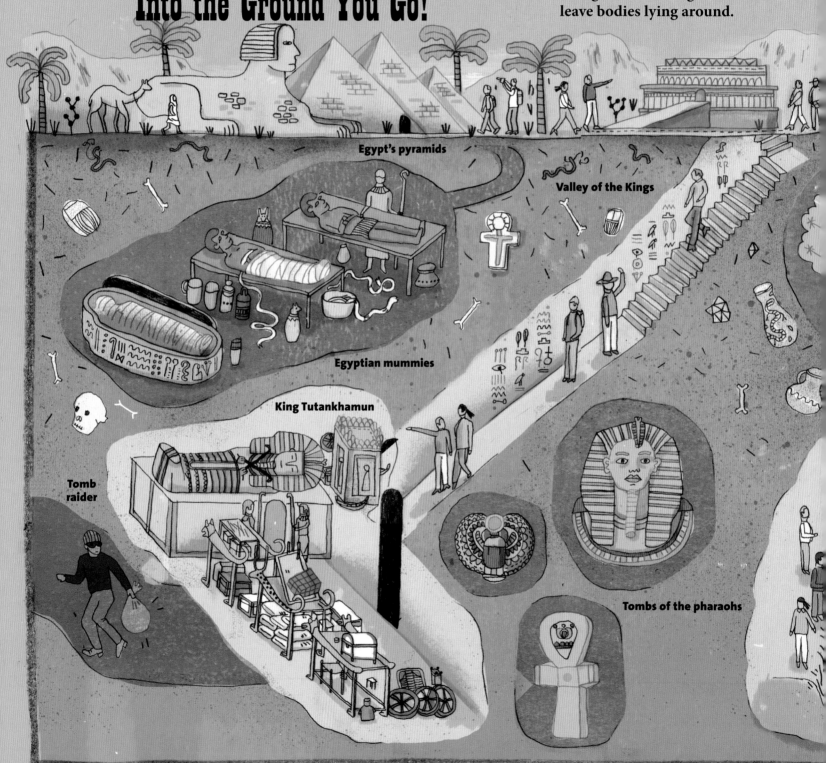

Egypt's pyramids

Valley of the Kings

Egyptian mummies

King Tutankhamun

Tomb raider

Tombs of the pharaohs

Emperor Qin's tomb

Terra-cotta warriors

Buried treasure at Sutton Hoo

TOMBS OF THE PHARAOHS

The first rulers of Egypt were entombed in the famous pyramids, but 1000 years later, pharaohs such as Ramesses V and Ramesses VI, Seti and Tutankhamun chose to be buried in hidden rock caves beneath the empty-looking Valley of the Kings. No one was ever meant to see these decorated underground rooms once they were sealed, but archaeologists have now been working in them for more than 200 years.

TOMB RAIDERS

All those riches hidden in pyramids and tombs were a great temptation to grave robbers. Most were broken into and emptied within 200 years, despite the fake doors, tunnels and staircases the builders put in to confuse raiders.

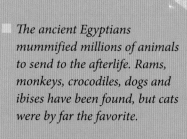

This empty jewelry box belonged to Tjuyu. Her tomb was uncovered in 1905, but tomb raiders had been there thousands of years earlier.

King Tut was buried with his favorite game.

Actually, I think I would've preferred the kennel.

PACKING FOR THE NEXT WORLD

The pharaohs loved to spend time packing for their deaths. They were buried with food, clothes, jewels, pets, games and tiny statues of servants to wait on them in the afterlife. This was an improvement on the earliest kings, who liked their own servants to be killed and buried with them.

The ancient Egyptians mummified millions of animals to send to the afterlife. Rams, monkeys, crocodiles, dogs and ibises have been found, but cats were by far the favorite.

ROYAL VALLEY

Steeply sloping rock corridors lead down through decorated rooms to the burial chamber of brothers Ramesses V and Ramesses VI.

More than 63 tombs have been discovered so far in the Valley of the Kings. Ancient Egypt's pharaohs chose to be buried here from 1600 BCE to 1100 BCE.

In ancient Egypt, tomb raiding was punished by torture, then death.

I'm a daddy, not a mummy. And where's my cat?

CALL ME MUMMY

Ancient Egyptians thought a body had to be buried intact for the soul to survive and enjoy the afterlife. Since dead bodies decompose, they invented a way to preserve them: mummification. During mummification, most organs were removed — the brain was pulled out through the nose — and the embalmed body was wrapped in strips of linen.

■ *Tourists have been coming to the Valley of the Kings since Roman times.*

Graffiti in one tomb dates back to 273 BCE.

■ *The ancient Egyptians believed the gods of death — with the heads of jackals or black falcons — would collect the pharaoh from his tomb and lead him to Osiris, god of the afterlife.*

Tomb raiders didn't always have to dig through rock: sometimes they bribed the builders not to seal a tomb properly.

41

THE CURSE OF KING TUT?

> Who's a pretty ... AAAAGGH!

Some people believe that on the day that Carter discovered the mysterious steps, his pet canary was eaten by a royal cobra. Was this the first victim of the Mummy's Curse?

> Hmmm, steps leading down. It must be an ancient Metro station.

Archaeologists suspected there was another undiscovered tomb in the Valley of the Kings after a cup with the name "Tutankhamun" engraved on it was found. Howard Carter, a young English Egyptologist, was determined to find the tomb. Carter persuaded a rich friend, Lord Carnarvon, to fund his expedition in 1917.

1 Howard Carter dug for five years without luck. In 1922, Carnarvon agreed to pay for one last search. On November 4, Carter found 16 steps under an ancient hut; at the bottom was a door.

Scientists studied King Tut's feet and concluded that he suffered from a painful bone disorder in his right foot and club foot in his left.

> Curses! This feels very undignified ...

4 In the inner chamber was a stone sarcophagus containing three man-shaped coffins nested inside one another. The first two were wood; the innermost was solid gold and contained the mummy of King Tut.

"They who enter this sacred tomb shall swift be visited by wings of death."

A curse was said to be carved in hieroglyphics in the tomb (it wasn't). When Carnarvon died from an infected mosquito bite two months after the tomb was found, the Mummy's Curse was blamed.

Hmmm, who can I curse next?

Help, my hand's stuck!

2 Carter hid the steps and wrote to Carnarvon to come quickly. On November 26, the rich lord arrived for the grand opening of the tomb. Carter made a small hole in the top of the door and peered in with his candle.

3 The candle lit up piles of gold objects. The tomb was small, but it still held its treasures. The men spent months listing Tut's riches before they reached his burial chamber on February 16, 1923.

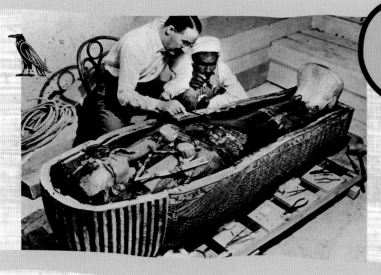

Get the lid on quick. I've made a bit of a mess in here.

5 The mummy was dressed in a solid gold death mask. Tut's liver, lungs, stomach and intestines were stored nearby in canopic jars. He was entombed with 413 tiny *shawabtis* — servant dolls that would wait on him in the afterlife.

6 Were Carter and Carnarvon doomed? There were rumors that the tomb builders had protected it with a curse. The mummy broke into pieces when Carter tried to take off the death mask.

QIN'S ARMY OF DEATH

JUST LIKE SNOWFLAKES ...

The terra-cotta warriors were all rather gray after 2000 years in the ground, but patches of paint on them tell archaeologists that they were once individually colored. Just like a real army, the soldiers all differ in height and weight — the smallest is 1.73 m (5 ft. 8 in.) and the tallest is 1.97 m (6 ft. 5.5 in.). Each has a different face, hairstyle, uniform and posture.

When a Chinese farmer named Yang Zhifa set out to dig a well outside the city of Xian in 1974, he had no idea an army was lined up in the ground beneath him. He discovered a life-size terra-cotta soldier, and a burial site where more than 7000 warriors stood at attention in the earth, each one poised for battle to defend his master.

Pull your stomach in, man!

THE MIGHTY QIN

The terra-cotta army was buried to protect the first Chinese emperor, Qin. He ordered 700 000 men to start working on his tomb when he took the throne in 246 BCE at age 13. Rather pessimistic, wasn't he?

THIS IS THE PITS

Most of the army was found in four pits. The warriors are divided into different fighting forces: chariot drivers, infantry, cavalry and archers. All were lined up facing east, where Qin's enemies lived.

Qin's burial mound is located close to where the warriors were found. It hasn't been excavated, but ancient writings describe it as filled with model palaces and cities. Rivers of mercury flow through bronze hills, which are decorated with jewels.

WARRIOR ASSEMBLY LINE

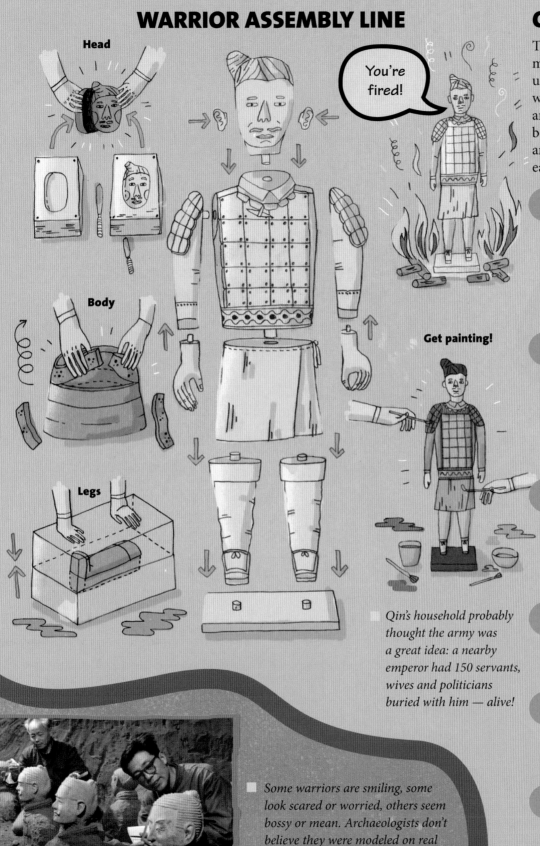

Head

Body

Legs

You're fired!

Get painting!

Qin's household probably thought the army was a great idea: a nearby emperor had 150 servants, wives and politicians buried with him — alive!

Some warriors are smiling, some look scared or worried, others seem bossy or mean. Archaeologists don't believe they were modeled on real men, but they give us a good idea of how people looked then.

CLAYMATION

The emperor wanted so many soldiers that clay was used to make them — it was quick and cheap and each part could be made separately and joined together easily.

1 **Head**
The front and back of the head were made in two different molds, then joined together.

2 **Face and hair**
Molded clay beards and mustaches were stuck on or carved in. Hairstyles had to match the rank of the soldier: top knot, bun or braid.

3 **Body, arms and legs**
These were made separately then joined. A layer of clay was put over the top and clothing and armor details were carved into it.

4 **Firing**
The figures were fired at 1000°C (1832°F) to make them hard and tough. That worked!

5 **Painting**
Paint was mixed with egg to make it last. That didn't work as well!

6 **Armed and ready**
The soldiers were all buried with real weapons, but these were quickly stolen from the pits.

45

WHO'S HOO?

Imagine an enormous rowboat, 27 m (90 ft.) long, with 20 masked oarsmen rowing on either side. A longboat like this was used as a burial place for an Anglo-Saxon king 1300 years ago. The wooden boat dissolved into the soil long ago, but its imprint could clearly be seen by archaeologists, who found it while digging under a burial barrow (mound of earth) at Sutton Hoo in Suffolk, England, in 1939. There was no sign of a skeleton, but scientists tested the earth and found chemical traces of a human body that had been buried in the boat.

BURIED TREASURE

The warrior's precious possessions were buried with him in the ship. A masked iron helmet, decorated with bronze, was found in tiny pieces and rebuilt by archaeologists. A collection of items, including spears, a Viking-style round shield, armor, a sword decorated with gold and garnets, a gold belt buckle, a tunic shoulder clasp and a purse lid, had been laid by the body.

HOO'S CLUES

The armor and weapons buried with the body tell us that the dead person was likely a man. The jewels and decorated helmet show he was a rich and powerful warrior leader. That he was buried in his ship implies his beliefs were pagan, rather than Christian. He was buried with belongings from foreign lands, such as coins from the kingdom of the Franks and Mediterranean-style cloth, which tells archaeologists that he had traveled overseas or traded with foreigners.

In the grave was a leather purse with 37 gold coins. They were from the land of the Franks, and dated between 575 and 620 CE, which suggests that the warrior was alive in that year.

A magnificent but rather scary helmet was placed next to the body. Each eyebrow ends in a tiny boar's head, and between the eyebrows is a dragon's head.

The ship was found buried under the largest of around 20 mounds at Sutton Hoo. Archaeologists found marks on the hull where the ship had been patched up.

It's taken me 25 art classes to make this shield. Touch it and I'll spear you!

Early rock star? The body was buried with a lyre — a sort of early guitar. Presumably the warrior was a good musician.

READY, REDWALD?

The warrior was probably a king of the Angles of eastern England. The first Anglian king was Wuffa (not a noisy dog, but "The Wolf"), and the most famous was Redwald. The Anglian royal household was at Rendlesham, only a few kilometers/miles from Sutton Hoo. Redwald was so powerful that he became High King of all England. Archaeologists believe it is his body that was buried at Sutton Hoo. He died around 625 CE and, although he had become a Christian, his wife had persuaded him to keep worshipping pagan gods, too.

DEATH MARKS

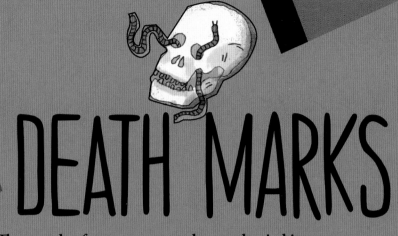

Thousands of years ago, people were buried in groups, under burial mounds or in large mass tombs. In modern times, we like a bit of privacy — most of us use one box (coffin) for each body and mark the grave in some way. But, just because someone's buried in the ground doesn't always mean it's the end of his or her story.

■ *Mourners wear black at funerals as a disguise so if any spirits come back from the dead, they won't be recognized.*

■ *In some countries, graves can be rented for only a specific period of time.*

A GRAVE EVENT

Today, most people have their name and dates written on their gravestone, but some like to have a last laugh. The gravestone of British comedian Spike Milligan reads: "I told you I was ill."

FOR RENT

PRACTICE MAKES PERFECT

Two hundred years ago, graveyards in the United Kingdom had a big problem ... body snatchers. Unscrupulous gangs would steal just-buried corpses and sell them to medical schools for trainee doctors to practice on. Family members stood guard over graves until the 1832 Anatomy Act put an end to body snatching.

■ *The body of silent-film star Charlie Chaplin was stolen from its grave in Switzerland in 1978. His widow, Lady Oona, received a ransom demand for £400 000 (around $600 000). The grave robbers thought their plan was foolproof, but Oona was no fool: she refused to pay up because Charlie would have thought it "ridiculous."*

In parts of Turkmenistan, rows of goat horns stick up out of the ground to mark graves.

I've never heard anything so ridiculous, darling.

MEXICAN DAY OF THE DEAD

Even the dead and buried can still enjoy a good party. Mexico's Day of the Dead celebrations actually last for three days each year, starting on October 31. Souls of dead children come up to party on November 1, and adult ghostly guests arrive on November 2.

1 **First day**
Relatives take food to Mexican cemeteries and sit on rugs on the ground to celebrate with the dead. They clean the graves and decorate them with orange marigolds.

GET ME OUT!

In the 19th century, people were so scared of being buried alive that they paid for special coffins. Some had waving flags or tiny bell towers above ground, with ropes inside for the "dead body" to raise the alarm if it woke up.

There is only enough air in a coffin to last for one hour, however many alarm bells it has.

2 **Second day**
Private altars in homes are decorated with pictures of the dead and their favorite things — like a scrapbook of memories. Friends drop by to eat sugar skulls.

I can't wait to get back into my cozy coffin.

Some people believe that vampires are people who were buried alive.

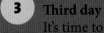

3 **Third day**
It's time to hit the town! Parades and floats of costumed characters sing and dance. Groups of revelers carry coffins with people dressed up as skeletons inside.

CHAPTER 5

Hide-and-Seek

Dig Deep and Keep Quiet

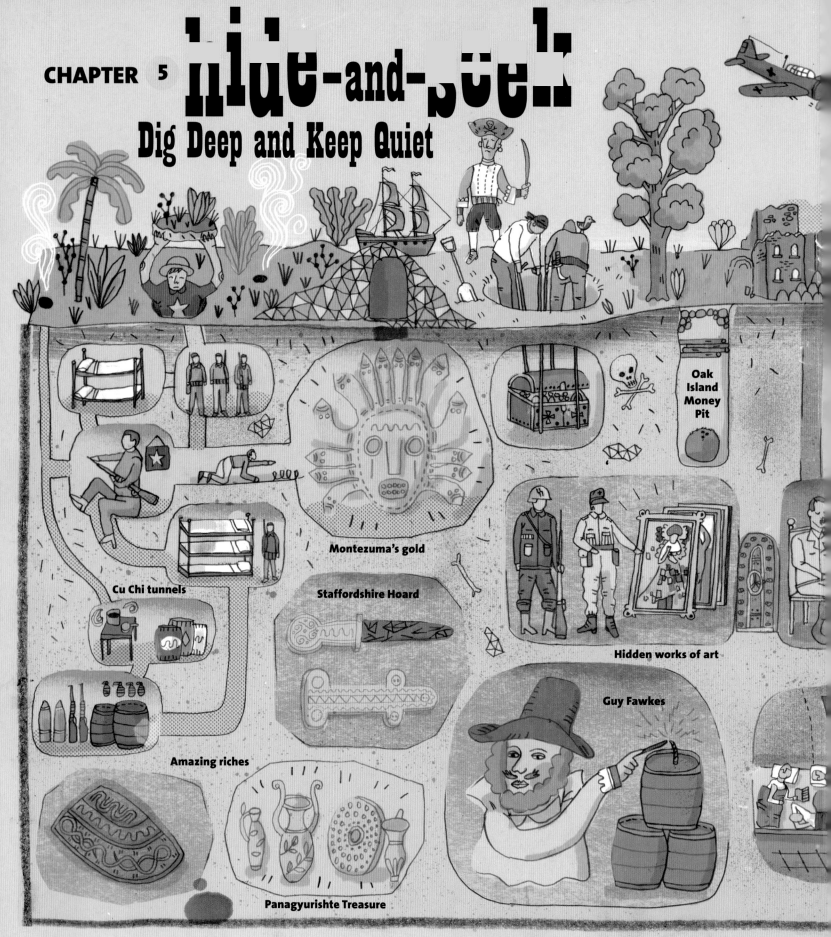

Cu Chi tunnels

Montezuma's gold

Staffordshire Hoard

Oak Island Money Pit

Hidden works of art

Guy Fawkes

Amazing riches

Panagyurishte Treasure

The underworld is a truly invisible hiding place, and not just for treasure. For thousands of years, people have hidden themselves underground to stay safe or to surprise an enemy.

Medieval castle pantry

War office

Hitler's bunker

Wartime hospital

Secret tunnel

Londoners during the Blitz

Torture chamber

BURIED TREASURE

Pirates steal treasure, then bury it in the ground and carry a map with a big *X* on it to mark the spot, right? Wrong. Only one pirate, Captain William Kidd, is known to have buried treasure — the rest never let it out of their sweaty grasp. But gold and jewels *have* been hidden underground for thousands of years by scared people unable to carry them because they were fleeing from enemies or natural disasters.

Dig Here! ✗

Start

■ *Pirate Captain William Kidd buried chests of gold and gems near New York in 1699, but police dug them up.*

HELLO AGAIN

The Bactrian Treasure has been discovered twice. This hoard of 20 000 pieces of gold jewelry from 100 CE was dug up in 1978 in Afghanistan. It was hidden in a secret vault when the Soviets invaded in 1979 and only rediscovered in 2003.

PIRATE TREASURE

In the 15th century, the powerful Spanish Empire mined gold and silver in South America and shipped it home as dollar coins, called "pieces of eight." The ships were often robbed by pirates, who then kept their hoard safe until they were ready to trade.

THE MONEY PIT

This is a long-running treasure hunt ... In 1795, three boys discovered a deep pit on Oak Island in Nova Scotia. Over the course of several years, they dug to a depth of nearly 30 m (90 ft.), where they found a stone with an inscription that was translated as: "Forty feet below, 2 million pounds are buried." Shortly after they found the stone, the pit flooded and collapsed. People are still digging there today.

STAFFORDSHIRE HOARD

It seems amazing that treasure can stay hidden under somewhere as busy as England, but the Staffordshire Hoard of 7th-century gold and silver weapons and jewels lay silently under the English city of Lichfield until it was discovered in 2009.

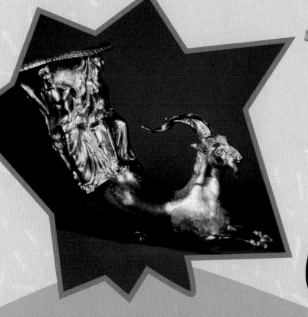

BROTHERS IN LUCK

In December 1949, near the Bulgarian village of Panagyurishte, three brothers digging for clay to make tiles found a hoard of nine heavy gold drinking vessels made in 400 BCE by the Thracians. Historians think the treasure is a dining set that belonged to the Thracian royal family.

MONTEZUMA'S GOLD

This treasure is a famous legend of Mexico and the southern United States. Montezuma was a super-rich Aztec emperor who greeted Spaniard Hernán Cortés with generous gold and silver gifts. He thought Cortés was a god, but Cortés was actually coming to invade. After Montezuma's death, the legend of his vast treasures being buried in the ground began.

DEADLY DUNGEONS

Some medieval castles had prison cells beneath them, complete with torture chambers for persuading prisoners to say what the jailer wanted to hear. These dungeons usually had very thick walls and were very dimly lit — well, they had just enough light for the prisoner to see the torturer, face covered with a black hood, and the heads of previous victims on spikes.

- *Underground was the best place for gunpowder, for obvious reasons! Nobody wanted nasty accidents caused by stray cannonballs hitting the barrels.*

- *Torture by rat was popular in dungeons because it was cheap and easy: rats were everywhere! In this method of torture, the rats would be persuaded to eat their way through the victim's body.*

Hungry, hungry, hungry ...

UNDER-FLOOR STORE

Most castles didn't actually have horrible, dark dungeons; they had something much less scary beneath them: a big pantry. In the days before fridges, food was stored in huge stone cellars under castle kitchens to prevent it from turning bad. The castle's store of gunpowder was kept below ground, too, as well as any hoards of treasure that needed to be hidden from enemies.

Now, don't go hopping off anywhere.

TOTAL TORTURE

The iron maiden was a torture device that some people believe was used in the 16th century. A criminal was tied inside and the doors were shut. The spikes on the inside of the doors would stab into the victim, but they were carefully arranged to miss all of his or her vital organs, so he or she died slowly in complete darkness.

FORGOTTEN FOREVER

Medieval prisoners were sometimes kept in an *oubliette*, which comes from the French word for "forgotten." This was a dungeon with a tiny, man-size hole in the ceiling. The prisoner was lowered in through a hatch and never came out again — he or she was just left there until everyone forgot about him or her.

ROBBER BARON

In the 15th century, Knight Erazem Lueger of Slovenia was besieged in his castle for a year by the Habsburg army. He taunted the soldiers by pelting them with fresh cherries. How could he get food if he was besieged? A secret tunnel under the castle led to the village so he could sneak out to do his shopping.

After all those cherries, I'm off to the bathroom!

The robber baron came to a messy end. He was hit by a single cannonball while enjoying private time in the bathroom at the top of a castle tower.

The rack was a popular torture device in the Middle Ages. The victim's wrists and ankles were tied to handles with ropes. When the handles were turned, the ropes pulled until the victim's bones dislocated with a loud crack.

In torture by goat, the victim's feet are dipped in salty water, which is licked off by a goat. At first the licking tickles, then it becomes painful, and finally, when the goat licks away layers of skin, it's torture!

LIFE IN THE TRENCHES

Soldiers in World War I spent a lot of time underground. German troops marched into France and came face-to-face with the Allies. The land was flat and the only way to take cover was to dig into the ground. Within months, parallel lines of deep ditches called "trenches" stretched for hundreds of kilometers/miles. The German and Allied trenches were opposite each other, with a space called "no-man's-land" in the middle.

BOGGED DOWN

Because the Germans were the first to dig trenches, they picked the best spots. Some Allied trenches were on low ground and flooded whenever it rained. Shell holes filled with water deep enough for soldiers to drown in.

GOING OVER THE TOP

There was only one thing worse than being in the trenches, and that was coming out of the trenches. Officers would decide when it was time for the soldiers to try to gain land by "going over the top." This was often fatal.

HAPPY RATS

Rats also found homes in the trenches. They fed on soldiers' food rations and on the dead bodies that lay across no-man's-land. Some grew as large as cats.

NOT SO SNUG

Each soldier would have his own little bedroom in the trench ... but not a bedroom like you have at home. The soldiers' dugouts were grave-sized burrows off the main trench, reinforced with planks and sandbags to stop the roof from caving in. The soldier could hang up a blanket to give himself some privacy.

TRENCH TOWN

The German trenches were usually better built than the Allied trenches. Some were 2–3 m (6–9 ft.) deep and run like a mini town, with command rooms and hospitals.

■ *The Allies also used underground command bunkers, but theirs tended to be cramped and uncomfortable.*

They may have better trenches, but we'll beat them in the end.

SHELL SHOCK

Many soldiers who spent time in the trenches were never the same again — they returned home with shell shock. After living in a ditch of rats and lice, with bombs exploding around them and the enemy hiding nearby, ready to fire, many of them were nervous and scared for the rest of their lives.

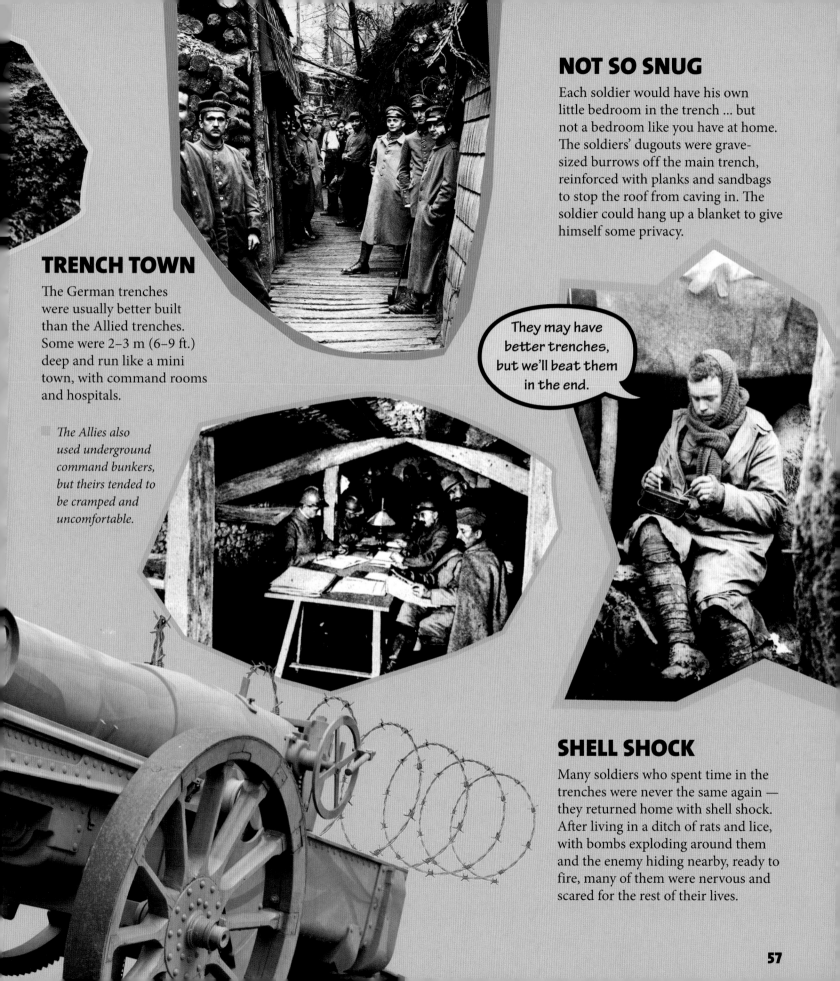

I wondered where that Picasso painting had got to.

BLITZ BEDS

During the Blitz bombings of World War II, people slept in London's Underground stations. At first, the government banned sleeping in the Tube, but everyone just bought cheap tickets to get in, then refused to come out until breakfast.

■ *During World War II, England's prime minister, Winston Churchill, had an underground war office.*

■ *Nazi armies stole treasures and paintings from museums across Europe and hid them in salt mines.*

THIS MEANS WAR

When bombs are dropping from the sky and soldiers are creeping around with loaded guns, underground hiding places are used for defense and attack. Plans are made, armies are fed and hidden and valuables are stored ... underground.

LAST SEEN HERE ...

Nazi leader Adolf Hitler spent the last six months of his life in this concrete bunker, with his dog, Blondi, and his girlfriend, Eva Braun. Hitler and Braun married here and then committed suicide on April 30, 1945. Hitler's death signaled the end of World War II.

GUNPOWDER PLOTTERS

In 1604, Guy Fawkes and his Catholic friends hatched a plan to assassinate King James I of England by blowing up the Houses of Parliament. They started digging a tunnel from a nearby house, then found out there was a cellar for rent underneath the Parliament. They filled the cellar with gunpowder, but were caught before they lit the explosives.

CU CHI TUNNELS

During the Vietnam War, thousands of Viet Cong fighters hid from American troops in a 200 km (125 mi.) network of tunnels. They crawled through tiny trapdoors into narrow, stifling passages that led to underground villages with kitchens, dormitories and hospitals.

digging for riches
Treasures from the Earth

Children in coal mines

Open-pit mine

Coal mining in Roman times

Canary "gas alarms"

It didn't take us long to realize that the ground beneath our feet is a treasure trove. Coal and oil from underground can be used to make fire and create energy, and sparkling rocks and minerals can be traded or worn as jewelry.

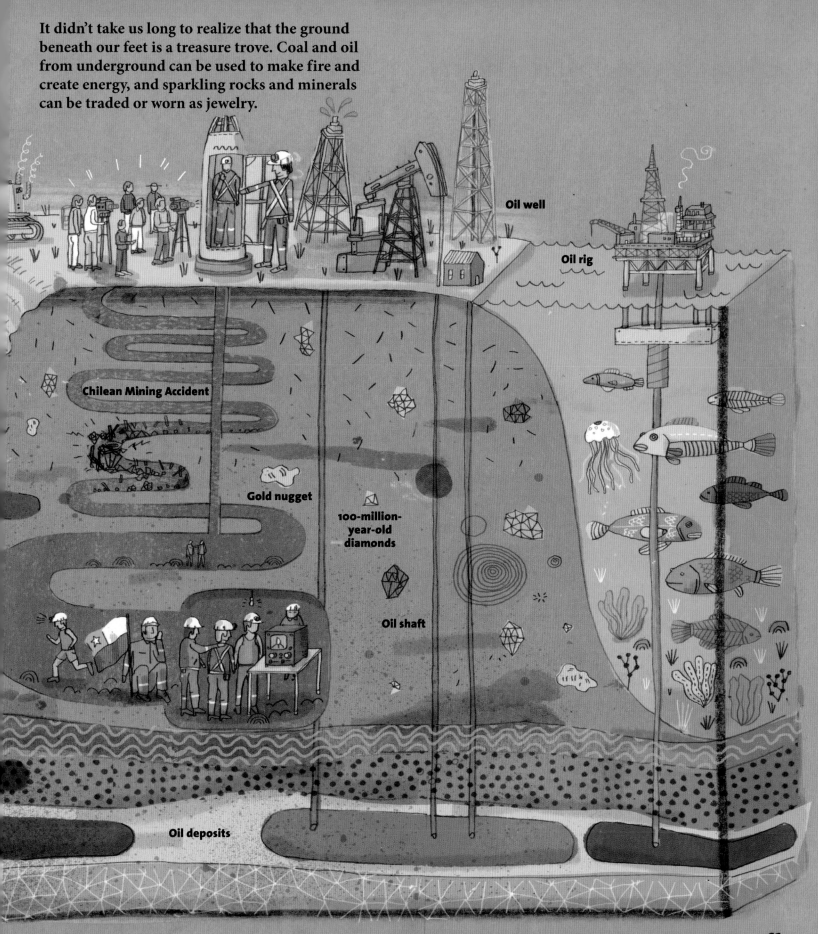

Oil well

Oil rig

Chilean Mining Accident

Gold nugget

100-million-year-old diamonds

Oil shaft

Oil deposits

MINE, MINE, MINE ...

There are plenty of natural riches under the ground, and it didn't take us long to discover them. Early humans perhaps noticed that, when they made fires, some bits of ground burned better than others. We know from ancient writings that 3000 years ago, the Chinese used special little black rocks to make fire: coal. And in 347 CE, the Chinese were pushing bamboo pipes 240 m (800 ft.) underground to drill for oil.

RICHES FOR ROMANS

The Romans dug mines all over their vast empire. Sometimes they even invaded countries they thought might be good to mine, such as Spain for its silver, or Wales for its gold (although only one Roman gold mine has ever been found there). They used water to wash away rock to find gold, or iron picks and hammers to dig below-ground tunnels.

I can't wait till they invent the backpack.

BUBBLING BAKU

One hundred years ago, Baku, Azerbaijan, was one of the world's largest oil producers. Marco Polo traveled here in the 12th century and saw this "fire water" being collected. You might never have heard of Baku, but this is where the first modern oil well was sunk, and by 1900 it produced half the world's supply. Even today, oily mud bubbles up out of the ground there in mini, belching oil volcanoes.

GOLD RUSH

In 1799, a 12-year-old boy named Conrad Reed found a huge, glittering rock on his father's farm in North Carolina. He took the 7.7 kg (17 lb.) gold nugget home and used it as a doorstop for three years before selling it to a jeweler. By 1849, thousands of people were rushing to the United States to try to dig up a gold fortune. Some didn't even have to dig — at first, gold nuggets could be found lying around on the ground.

In the days before alarm clocks, you couldn't say you overslept. The mine employed a "knocker-up" who walked around the village tapping on miners' windows with a long stick to wake them up.

Pit ponies were lowered into the mine and lived in underground stables. They came up once a year for the mine holiday.

KEEPING THE COAL COMING

When early people ran out of wood to burn, they discovered coal — in rivers and streams, then on hillsides. When they dug into a hillside, they found that the coal ran in a thick horizontal layer called a seam. Tunneling straight into the hillside was called drift mining, and it was very dangerous — the tunnels could collapse at any time. Eventually, mines became more sophisticated and deep shafts were dug straight down by machinery. The coal mine had jobs for the whole town, even children. By the end of the 19th century, many countries and regions had enacted laws prohibiting children from working in the mines.

In the days before elevators, coal was carried up the mine shaft in a large bucket. The miners would travel this way as well.

Small children were valued mine workers. They could open doorways and work in tiny spaces — and they didn't have to be paid much! Some stayed underground for 18 hours at a time.

I'm going to hold my breath. That'll teach you a lesson.

Air pockets in the mine were full of poisonous gases. Mines kept canaries as "gas alarms" — if a canary died, the miners took that as a warning.

UNDERGROUND INDUSTRY

Today's mines are built on a much larger scale than mines were during the early searches for gold or coal. Instead of digging by hand and crawling through narrow shafts, modern miners use explosives and drive huge vehicles down steep road tunnels deep into the earth. Open-pit miners blast away a layer of rock, remove the goodies, then blast away another layer, until a huge pit forms. Some mining companies even blast the tops off mountains.

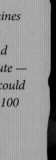

Why don't we just blast the top off this hill instead?

THAT'S A BIG HOLE

In 1871, South African miners started work on a diamond mine called "The Big Hole." They used shovels and picks and kept digging for more than 40 years (with lunch and coffee breaks), until they had dug down 240 m (800 ft.). This is still the deepest hand-dug pit in the world.

GOLD MANSION

In the whole of human history, we've dug more than 170 000 tonnes (187 000 tons) of gold out of planet Earth. If it were squashed together, all this gold would make a nugget about the size of a large house ... which doesn't really sound like that much gold, does it?

Some modern machines can dig out 5 tonnes (5.5 tons) of rock and minerals every minute — more than a miner could dig in an entire day 100 years ago.

■ *The Bagger 288 — a huge extractor that scoops out enormous buckets of coal — is one of the the biggest land vehicles in the world.*

BIG, BIGGER, BIGGEST

1 **Bingham Canyon copper mine** in Utah is the deepest open-pit mine in the world. It's 4 km (2.5 mi.) across and 1.2 km (0.75 mi.) deep. Copper has been dug out of here since 1906.

2 **Mirny diamond mine** in Russia is 525 m (1720 ft.) deep and 1.2 km (0.75 mi.) across. Helicopters are no longer allowed to fly over the hole in case they are sucked in by its strong downward air currents.

3 **TauTona gold mine** in South Africa is 3.9 km (2.4 mi.) deep — the deepest shaft mine in the world.

The Mirny open-pit diamond mine was closed in 2011.

The gem amethyst is a form of the mineral quartz. Its purple color is created by manganese in the quartz.

HIDDEN GEMS

ROCK STARS

Heat and pressure hundreds of kilometers/miles underground create a diamond from tiny atoms of carbon. Diamonds are the hardest natural minerals on the planet, which is a bit odd when you realize that the carbon they're made from can also turn into graphite — the softest mineral on the planet!

It's hard to imagine, but gemstones such as diamonds, rubies and emeralds are formed underground. Most gemstones are crystals, but most crystals are not gemstones. It takes a special sort of crystal to be cut and polished into a gem and used for trading or jewelry.

Diamonds aren't always clear. A diamond can be pink, blue, yellow, orange, purple, green or even black, depending on what other minerals were involved when it was formed.

The Hope Diamond is a huge blue diamond said to be a curse to its owner. Marie Antoinette once wore it. Perhaps that's why she lost her head!

BLUE RUBIES

Despite their special redness or blueness, rubies and sapphires are actually twins. Two hundred years ago, scientists discovered that both are varieties of corundum, the world's second-hardest mineral. Pure corundum is clear, red corundum is called a ruby and all other colors are called sapphires.

HOLY EMERALD!

The pharaohs of Egypt mined emeralds near the Red Sea 5000 years ago. Archaeologists discovered their mines in the 19th century, but they were completely empty — the Egyptians had dug up all the emeralds. The Incas and Aztecs also thought the bright green emerald was a holy gem.

JEWELS IN THE CROWN

Britain's Crown Jewels are kept in the Tower of London under armed guard. It's not surprising when you learn that the Imperial State Crown alone contains 2868 diamonds, 17 sapphires, 11 emeralds and 5 rubies. The Star of Africa, which rests on top of the Sovereign's Scepter, is the second-largest cut diamond in the world.

The huge Koh-i-Noor diamond is mounted on Britain's Imperial State Crown. It was mined in India, but seized by the East India Company in 1849 and given to Queen Victoria.

Only one person has tried to steal the jewels — Irish Colonel Thomas Blood, in 1671. Blood's gang overpowered the Tower's gatekeeper and hid a crown and scepter in their breeches. They were only foiled when the gatekeeper's son returned unexpectedly.

CAVE IN: RESCUING "THE 33"

When the first miner came up alive after 69 days underground, Chile celebrated and the world watched on TV.

Working underground is very dangerous. Tunnels can collapse at any time, leaving miners crushed or buried under rock in pockets of air. The world's worst mining accident was in 1942, when 1549 miners died in a coal mine in China.

In August 2010, disaster struck at a 121-year-old mine deep below Chile's Atacama Desert, one of the driest places on Earth. On Thursday, August 5, a cave-in at the San José mine buried 33 men 700 m (2300 ft.) below ground. The thick dust cloud caused by the rockfall blinded the men for six hours.

On August 22, video cameras were sent down the boreholes and the miners could be seen for the first time since the cave-in 17 days earlier.

ORDER OF EVENTS

1 A rockfall leaves 33 men buried 700 m (2300 ft.) below ground in a mine, 5 km (3 mi.) from the mine's entrance, down a long, steep, winding underground roadway.

2 Everyone assumes the men haven't survived the cave-in and that even if they have survived, they will starve to death below ground before they can be rescued.

3 The 33 men take refuge in an emergency shelter with enough food for two days. Their leader, Luis Urzúa, gives them all jobs and takes charge of sharing the rations.

4 Above ground, rescuers start drilling eight boreholes into the ground.

5 Seventeen days after the accident, one of the drills breaks into the tunnel where the men are sheltering. They attach a note in big red letters to the end of the drill bit: "We are well in the shelter, the 33."

6 The men are discovered just after their meager rations run out. The drill hole is enlarged enough to pass glucose drinks, food, letters and gifts down to the men.

THE RACE TO RESCUE

Once the miners were discovered alive, emergency crews had to figure out how to rescue them. The Chilean government took advice from all over the world and mining experts arrived at the site to help. Camp Hope was set up at the surface, where kitchens, bathrooms and eventually even a school were built for the miners' families.

August 30
The rescuers don't know what will work so they start drilling three different holes.

September 24
The miners have been alive below ground for 50 days — a world record.

October 9
Drill B reaches the miners. It is used to enlarge the communication borehole from 14 cm (5.5 in.) to 71 cm (28 in.).

October 12
An escape capsule, Phoenix, is lowered into the mine, taking 18 minutes to reach the miners. The first miner is slowly raised to the surface.

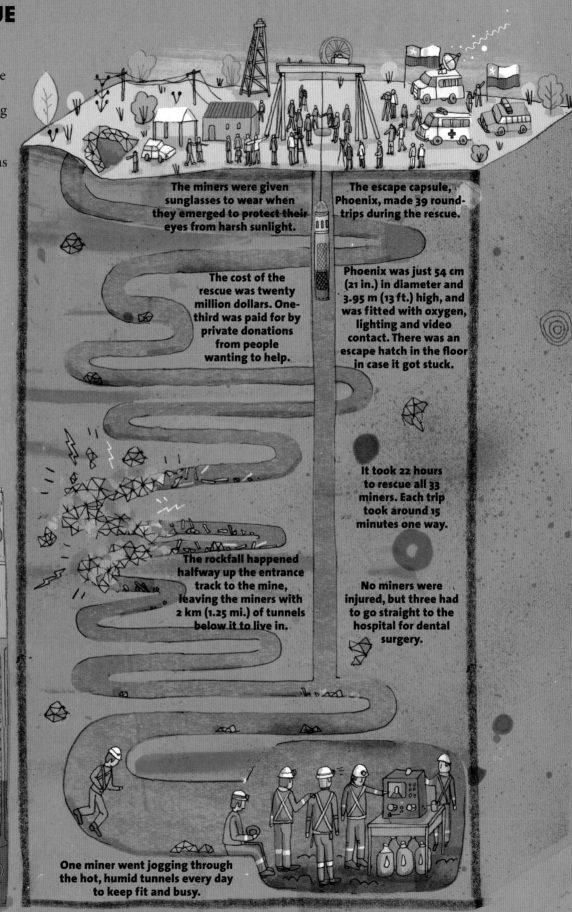

The miners were given sunglasses to wear when they emerged to protect their eyes from harsh sunlight.

The escape capsule, Phoenix, made 39 round-trips during the rescue.

The cost of the rescue was twenty million dollars. One-third was paid for by private donations from people wanting to help.

Phoenix was just 54 cm (21 in.) in diameter and 3.95 m (13 ft.) high, and was fitted with oxygen, lighting and video contact. There was an escape hatch in the floor in case it got stuck.

It took 22 hours to rescue all 33 miners. Each trip took around 15 minutes one way.

The rockfall happened halfway up the entrance track to the mine, leaving the miners with 2 km (1.25 mi.) of tunnels below it to live in.

No miners were injured, but three had to go straight to the hospital for dental surgery.

One miner went jogging through the hot, humid tunnels every day to keep fit and busy.

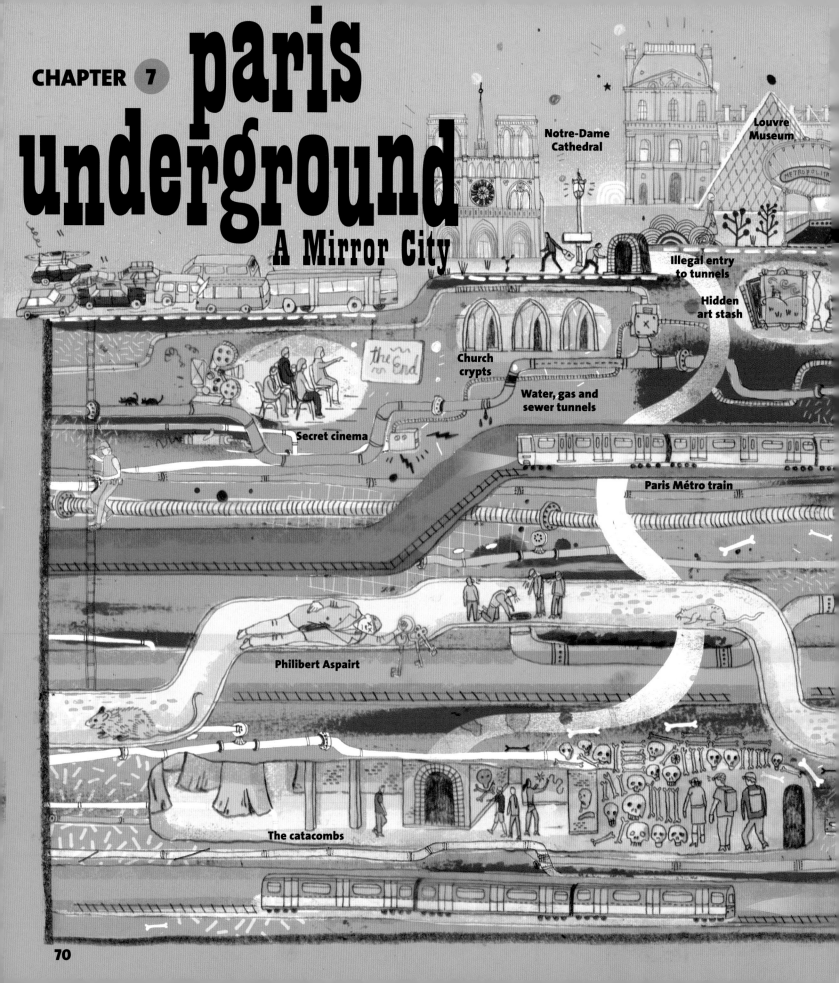

paris underground
A Mirror City

Notre-Dame Cathedral

Louvre Museum

Illegal entry to tunnels

Hidden art stash

Church crypts

the End

Secret cinema

Water, gas and sewer tunnels

Paris Métro train

Philibert Aspairt

The catacombs

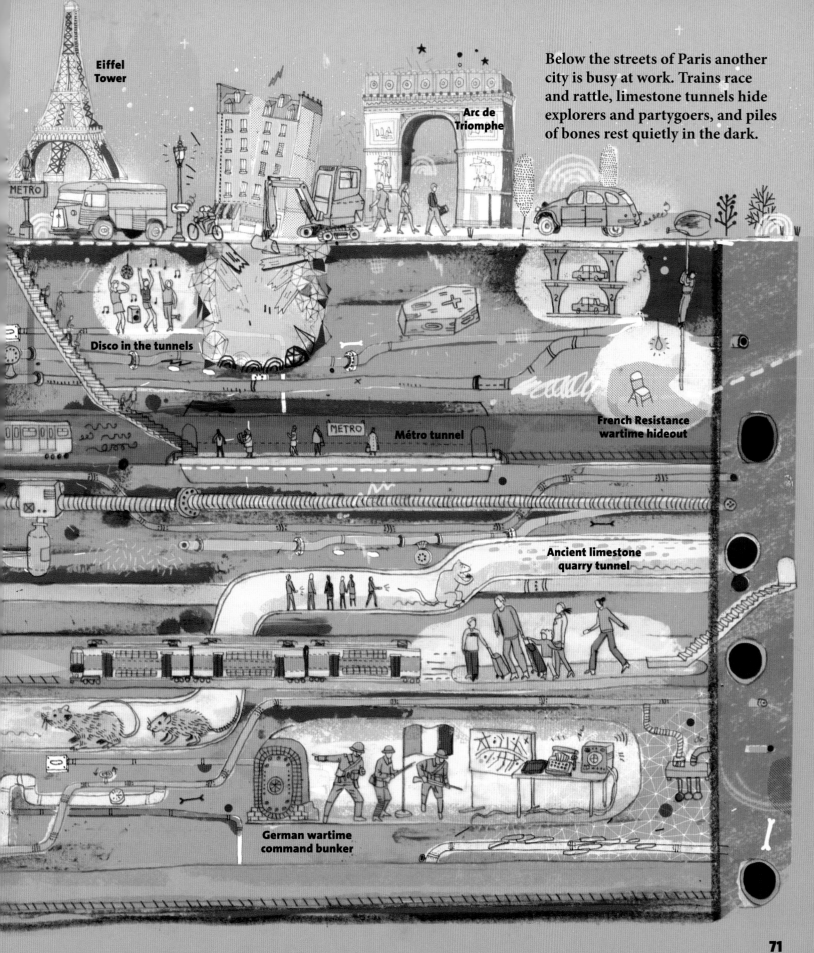

Eiffel
Tower

Arc de
Triomphe

METRO

Below the streets of Paris another
city is busy at work. Trains race
and rattle, limestone tunnels hide
explorers and partygoers, and piles
of bones rest quietly in the dark.

Disco in the tunnels

French Resistance
wartime hideout

METRO

Métro tunnel

Ancient limestone
quarry tunnel

German wartime
command bunker

A HIDDEN WORLD

Paris is nicknamed the "City of Light," but beneath it is an underground city so dark you can't see your hand in front of your face. More than a hundred miles of tunnels run under Paris, and centuries of history can be seen in them (if you've got a strong flashlight, that is). Underneath Paris are quarries that spread out in one of the longest mazes in the world, canals and sewers, crypts and bank vaults, prisons and bunkers, wine cellars converted into nightclubs, and even a secret underground cinema. There are hidden entrances to these tunnels all over the city, but many have been bricked up.

WHAT'S THAT SMELL?

Sewers are the pipes that carry away whatever you flush down your toilet. Paris's first underground sewer was built in 1370 — it must have been very simple, because toilets hadn't even been invented at that point.

In 1793, Philibert Aspairt, the doorkeeper of the Val-de-Grâce hospital, disappeared in the tunnels. His body was found 11 years later, near a doorway. His skeleton hands were still holding a set of keys — he just couldn't find the door in the dark.

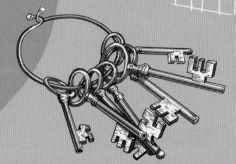

TUNNELS OF STONE

From the first days of the city of Paris, the rock beneath it has been mined to build the city above. The Louvre Museum and Notre-Dame Cathedral were built from this limestone. The tunnels of Paris run underneath bank vaults and prisons, so today they have their own police force to keep criminals from using them.

BASTILLE BEEHIVE

Paris is famous for its prisons and dungeons. The Bastille was the most famous prison of all. As well as being the spot where the French Revolution began, it was also home to a beehive-shaped *oubliette* dungeon. The only way in was through a hatch high up in the wall. The prisoner was lowered in by a rope, and his food and water was sent in the same way — as long as someone remembered he was in there!

■ In 1984, Paris sewer workers discovered something quite amazing but rather scary — a Nile crocodile had found its way into the 2000 km (1250 mi.) of sewers and was surviving happily on a diet of rats and city rubbish.

■ By the time of the French Revolution, the dungeons below the Bastille were so dirty and rat-infested that they couldn't even be used for prisoners.

I feel way out of my depth in this job.

Some of the tunnels have street signs that match the roads above, but most are unmapped. It's easy to get lost in the darkness. Since 1955, it has been illegal to enter the tunnels without a guide.

Many of the passageways underneath Paris are too low or narrow for a person to enter. Some flow with (rather stinky) water.

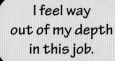

73

ENTRÉE DES CATACOMBES

1 **Place Denfert-Rochereau** — the entrance to the catacombs.

FULL TO BURSTING

In 1780, the cemeteries of Paris were full — in fact, one of the cemetery walls burst, spilling bones into a neighboring building. At the same time, the old quarry tunnels under the city were starting to cave in. Hmmm — maybe the two problems could be solved together? Over the next few years, many of the bones from Parisian cemeteries were moved to the quarries and the Paris catacombs became a gruesome tourist site.

THE CATACOMBS OF PARIS

The catacombs hold the skeletons of more than 6 million Parisians, stacked in 780 m (2560 ft.) of creepy underground corridors called an "ossuary." At first, the bones were simply thrown in, but soon the Parisians started to decorate the passages — not with paint and flower arrangements, but with neat displays of skulls and long bones.

6 Turning the corner, the corridor widens into a chapel known as the **Sacellum Crypt,** which contains an altar that looks like an ancient tomb.

5 The Cross of Stone

7 **The Sepulchral Lamp** is the oldest artifact in the catacombs. This is a huge bowl where the quarry workers kept a fire lit at all times. As well as giving light, the hot air from the fire made breezes, which forced air around the stuffy passageways.

2

A passageway leads 20 m (65 ft.) down below the city, getting colder and darker along the way.

3 A sculpture of a Spanish jail is carved into the tunnel wall near the entrance. It was made by Décure, a quarryman who was once a wartime prisoner of the English in this fortress jail.

4

The door to the ossuary is made of two large, decorated stone pillars. Written above the door in French are the words: "Stop! This is the empire of death."

9

The wall of skulls in the Crypt of the Passion hides a pillar that holds up the ceiling of the catacombs. Best not to lean against it ...

OSSEMENTS DU CIMETIÈRE DES INNOCENTS DÉPOSÉS EN AVRIL 1786

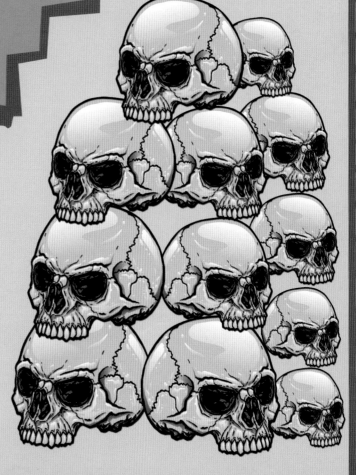

8 A special sign marks the spot where the first bones from Paris's biggest cemetery — the Cemetery of Innocents — were piled up in 1786.

THE PARIS MÉTRO

Under the busy streets of Paris, the Métro railway system carries 4.5 million people every day. Trains rush into and out of stations under the feet of pedestrians above — and not very far under the feet: a lot of the lines were dug directly under roads and then covered over. Paris has the second-busiest metro system in Europe, after Moscow. The first line opened on July 19, 1900.

Because many of the Métro lines were dug underneath roads, a map of the railway looks like a map of Paris above.

> Hmmm, City of Light above, City of Dark below. Cool!

CITY SYMBOL

Much of the Métro was built in the early 20th century. Many of the entrances were decorated in the Art Nouveau style that was all the rage in Paris then. Artists of this time liked to use colored glass and swirling curls of cast iron that look like jewelry. The decorated Métro signs have become a symbol of Paris.

Rather than tunneling under the ground, the builders of the Métro used the quicker "cut and cover" method. They dug up existing roads by hand, built a railway line beneath them, then covered them over again.

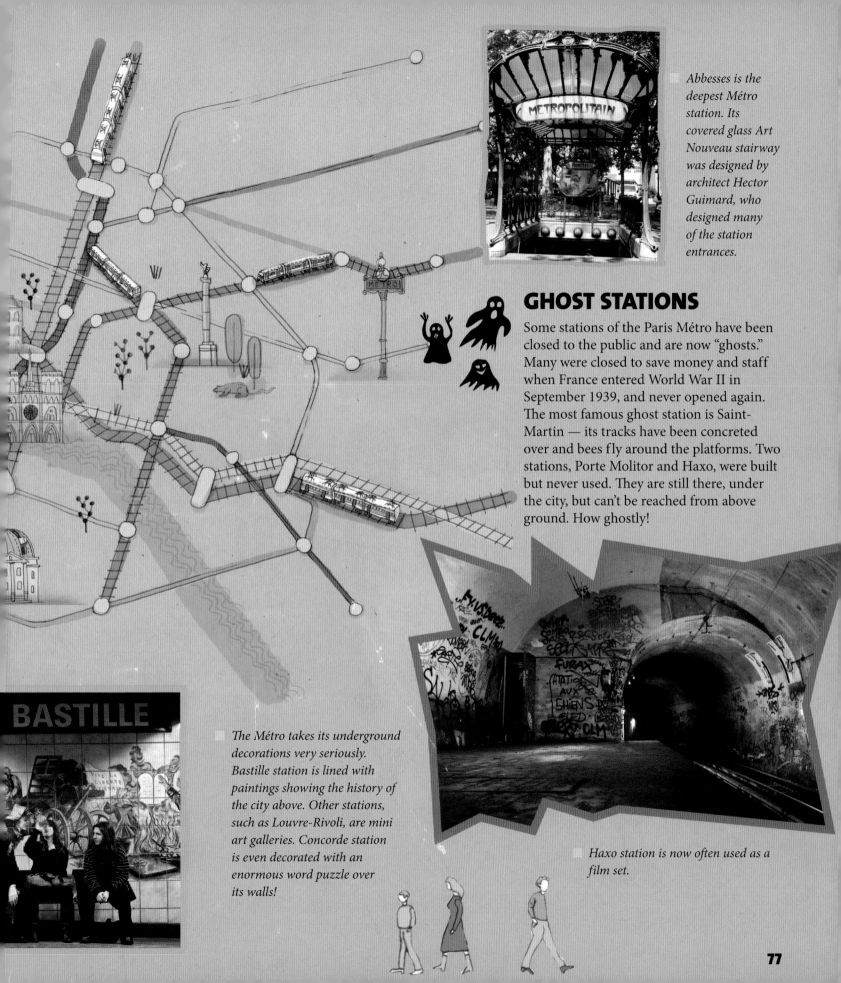

Abbesses is the deepest Métro station. Its covered glass Art Nouveau stairway was designed by architect Hector Guimard, who designed many of the station entrances.

GHOST STATIONS

Some stations of the Paris Métro have been closed to the public and are now "ghosts." Many were closed to save money and staff when France entered World War II in September 1939, and never opened again. The most famous ghost station is Saint-Martin — its tracks have been concreted over and bees fly around the platforms. Two stations, Porte Molitor and Haxo, were built but never used. They are still there, under the city, but can't be reached from above ground. How ghostly!

The Métro takes its underground decorations very seriously. Bastille station is lined with paintings showing the history of the city above. Other stations, such as Louvre-Rivoli, are mini art galleries. Concorde station is even decorated with an enormous word puzzle over its walls!

Haxo station is now often used as a film set.

tokyo underground

Nijubashi Bridge

Mode Gakuen Cocoon Tower

Tokyo Tower

Earthquake-proof architecture

Disaster Prevention Day

Common Utility Duct

"Underground Temple"

Tokyo Metro

Danger from Below

Tokyo is built on one of the most dangerous fault zones on Earth's crust. This modern city has to be prepared for danger from underground at all times.

Tokyo Skytree

Mount Fuji

Shopping center

Lava chamber to Mount Fuji

Subterranean farm

東京

Earth's plates colliding

Magma

MELTDOWN IN JAPAN

Japan is located in one of the most dangerous natural places on Earth, where three major tectonic plates rub and collide against one another. The slow, constant movement of these plates causes earthquakes. The Japanese have become accustomed to living with constant tremors and the threat of disaster.

FEAR OF FUJI

Japan has 10 percent of the world's active volcanoes. The most famous and highest volcano, Mount Fuji, can be seen from Tokyo. Mount Fuji last erupted in 1707 and it's said that if it erupted again, it would cause billions of dollars in damage. Fuji is currently resting quietly, but scientists have it wired up with early warning systems just in case.

In 1995, the Japanese city of Kobe was rocked by an earthquake.

THE RING OF FIRE

Where there are plate movements, there are usually volcanoes. A horseshoe-shaped danger zone called the Ring of Fire runs around the Pacific Ocean. Japan is inside this zone.

CITY SKYLINE

It's difficult to find an old building in Tokyo — the old architecture was destroyed on September 1, 1923, by the Great Kanto Earthquake. It is thought that 140 000 people died in the quake. The city was rebuilt using earthquake-proof architecture, and is now home to amazing futuristic towers.

NOT WAVING

A tsunami isn't like a surf wave that rises up, curls over and breaks on a beach. It's a powerful, moving, high wall of water created by an earthquake or eruption on the seabed.

The Great Wave at Kanagawa was painted around 1830. That's Mount Fuji in the background.

Tokyo

Japan's March 2011 earthquake registered 9 on the Richter Scale. Its tsunami was 7 m (23 ft.) high and flooded towns along Japan's coastline.

Keep to the left! This Japanese road cracked straight down the middle during an earthquake.

DID YOU FEEL THAT?

A seismograph measures the shaking of the ground. In 1935, Charles Richter invented a scale to rate and compare quakes. The strongest ever recorded was 9.5 in Chile in 1960.

ALWAYS BE PREPARED

Japan prides itself on being ready for anything. Every September 1 is Disaster Prevention Day. Local governments organize emergency drills, and all students and workers, even the prime minister, have to take part.

"UNDERGROUND TEMPLE"

It's not really a 21st-century temple — but with its high ceiling and forest of massive pillars, it certainly looks like one. Tokyo's surge chamber, right, is the largest human-made underground drainage system in the world. During Toyko's rainy season, water from the streets above runs down 10 m (32 ft.) wide tunnels into this chamber. From here, it's pumped out into the Edogawa River to prevent the city from flooding.

SCI-FI CITY

Other cities have ancient underground passages and tunnels, but descending into underworld Tokyo is like walking into a Star Wars movie. A network of passages links important government buildings and even an underground library.

Instead of stars, the ceiling of this underground walkway is lit by fluorescent lights.

NOT SO COMMON

A narrow spiral staircase leads to a massive shaft that plunges deep into Tokyo's underworld. The 20 m (66 ft.) wide concrete shaft drops down 40 m (130 ft.) to a tunnel that contains electric cables, telephone lines and gas and sewage pipes. This tunnel, right, is the Common Utility Duct, which protects Tokyo's cables and pipes in case of an earthquake.

SHOPPING FOR ...

Tokyo's Metro stations aren't just for trains. You can shop, eat, work and spend most of your life underground in this city, if you want. Tokyo's first subway line was built in 1927, and now more people ride Tokyo's underground trains than any other city's. Stations have their own shopping centers, and underground streets link to other Metro stations.

Shhh ... I think I can hear rain.

Shinjuku is the busiest train station in the world.

All those buildings and streets in busy Tokyo don't leave much green space for farms, so in 2005, the Japanese created Pasona O2. This underground farm has been planted in a 1000 m² (10 000 sq. ft.) disused bank vault under the city center.

THE SUBTERRANEAN FARM

NEITHER RAIN NOR SHINE

No sunlight or rain ever reaches the 100 different types of fruit and vegetables growing here under a 27-story tower. The temperature and special lights (different in each of the six rooms) are controlled by computer. Silver foil on the walls spreads the fluorescent light naturally. The farm wasn't set up to sell the food and flowers it grows — it doesn't produce enough for that. Instead, it was set up as a training school for young Japanese students who want to work as farmers.

1

Room 1 is a field of **flowers**. The farm is open to the public, so Tokyo workers can come and walk among the flowers.

■ *During the rice harvest, important Japanese businesspeople and leaders come downstairs to celebrate.*

2

Room 2 is where **herbs** are grown under metal spotlights.

3

Room 3 is the underground **terraced rice paddy,** which is harvested three times a year.

4

Room 4 is for **fruit and vegetables**. Tomatoes are grown by "hydroponics" — using water and little soil.

5

Room 5 is for **vegetables**. Broccoli, sprouts and cabbage? Hurray!

6

Room 6 is the **seedling room**. Baby lettuce grows under fluorescent lamps.

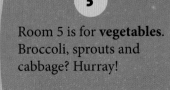

technotunnels

Our Future Underworld

The Large
Hadron Collider

Balaklava submarine base

Underground
government
mega-bunkers

Scientists working
underground

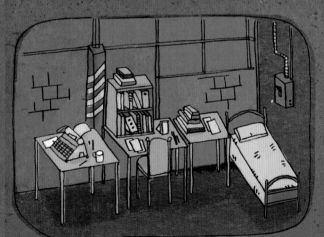

Burlington Bunker

Tagansky Protected
Command Point

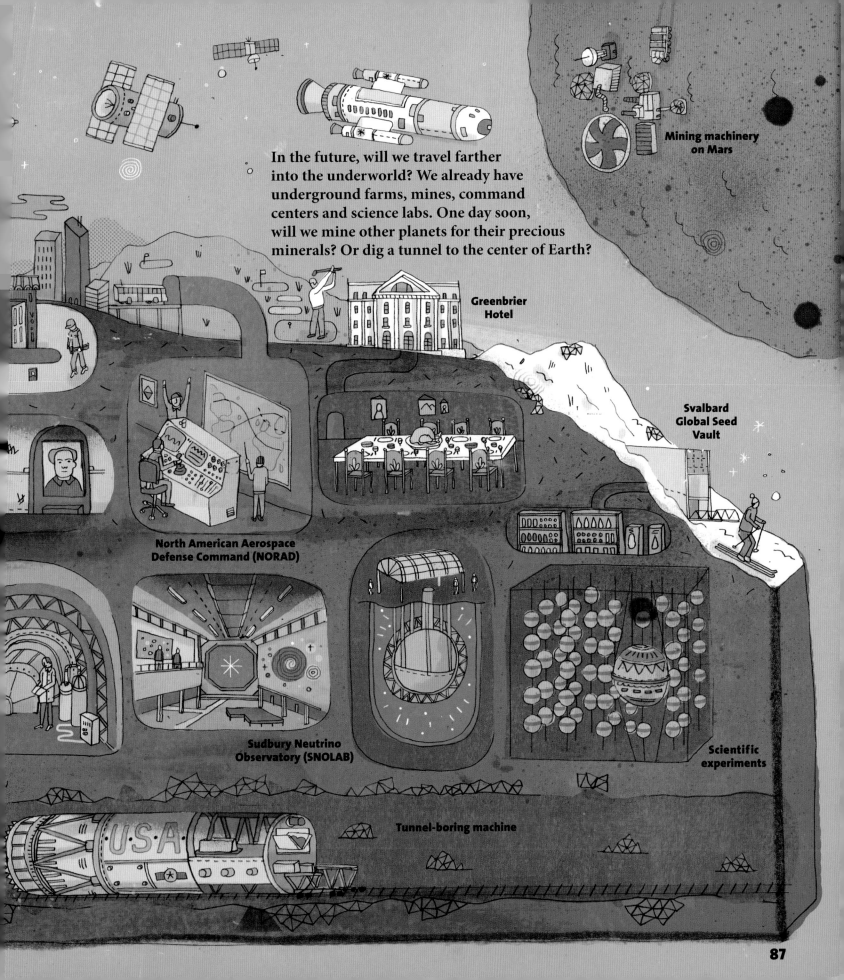

In the future, will we travel farther into the underworld? We already have underground farms, mines, command centers and science labs. One day soon, will we mine other planets for their precious minerals? Or dig a tunnel to the center of Earth?

Mining machinery on Mars

Greenbrier Hotel

Svalbard Global Seed Vault

North American Aerospace Defense Command (NORAD)

Sudbury Neutrino Observatory (SNOLAB)

Scientific experiments

Tunnel-boring machine

USA

DEEP SCIENCE

Why do scientists work underground to find signals from the rest of the universe? Because they need absolute silence and isolation from all the distracting noises, lights and messages flying around on Earth's crust for their experiments. The energy detectors scientists use are so sensitive that their results can be distorted by the cosmic rays that fall constantly on Earth's surface.

LOCATION: Below the border of France and Switzerland

DEPTH: 100 m (328 ft.)

STUDIES: Does the Higgs boson exist?

Below the Swiss border, scientists spent ten years building the Large Hadron Collider — the world's biggest machine. When it was switched on in 2008, people were scared it would create a black hole that could destroy the planet. Luckily, that didn't happen!

SOUDAN UNDERGROUND LABORATORY

LOCATION: Tower, Minnesota

DEPTH: 690 m (2264 ft.)

STUDIES: Do atoms decay? (Who cares? We all should because if atoms do decay — even after a trillion years — that's how long our universe will last!)

■ *The Soudan lab was built in an old iron mine.*

GRAN SASSO NATIONAL LABORATORY

■ *Gran Sasso is the largest underground physics lab in the world.*

LOCATION: Dug into the side of a 10 km (6 mi.) long motorway tunnel under Gran Sasso Mountain, Italy

DEPTH: 1400 m (4593 ft.)

STUDIES: Can neutrinos move faster than the speed of light? If the universe started with a Big Bang, could it end with a Big Crunch?

■ *The IceCube telescope at the South Pole searches for "neutrinos," mysterious fundamental particles that do not carry an electric charge.*

THE LARGE HADRON COLLIDER

■ *The tunnel is 27 km (17 mi.) long and kept at a temperature colder than outer space.*

The biggest machine was built to look for the tiniest particle in the universe — the Higgs boson "God particle." In July 2012, physicists at the LHC announced that they had found a particle consistent with the Higgs boson, and in March 2013, they confirmed that the particle was, in fact, a Higgs boson.

■ *Scientists know something is missing in the universe, but they don't know what. They call it "dark matter" and they are still trying to prove that it exists.*

BAKSAN NEUTRINO OBSERVATORY (BNO)

LOCATION: Deep in an abandoned mine, Baksan Gorge, Russia

DEPTH: 3.5 km (11 483 ft.)

STUDIES: What is the internal structure of the Sun and stars?

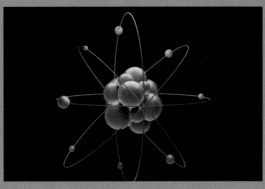

■ *Scientists at Baksan are trying to find out if a star creates a burst of neutrinos when it collapses.*

KAMIOKA OBSERVATORY (Super-K)

LOCATION: Kamioka-cho, Japan

DEPTH: 1 km (3281 ft.)

STUDIES: What are the properties of neutrinos? Can protons decay into lighter charged particles?

■ *Scientists at Kamioka have proved that neutrinos do have mass.*

SUDBURY NEUTRINO OBSERVATORY (SNOLAB)

■ *SNOLAB is a super-clean lab in an old mine.*

LOCATION: Sudbury, Ontario

DEPTH: 2 km (6562 ft.)

STUDIES: What is the nature of dark matter? Why does matter dominate over anti-matter in the universe?

NUCLEAR UNDERWORLD

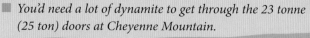

So, if World War III starts and nuclear missiles are fired, where will you go? Powerful people around the world have a plan for this emergency. Many countries have built secret mega-bunkers to keep their leaders safe, no matter what happens up above.

■ *You'd need a lot of dynamite to get through the 23 tonne (25 ton) doors at Cheyenne Mountain.*

BORING BUNKER

It may look like an old boarding school, but Burlington Bunker in Wiltshire, United Kingdom, was built for 4000 government ministers and staff to live in if there was a nuclear attack. This huge blast-proof, radiation-proof bunker is 30 m (100 ft.) below ground.

□ *Burlington Bunker has been abandoned since the early 1990s.*

UNDERGROUND CITY

Dixia Cheng is a 30 km (19 mi.) network of tunnels built in the 1970s beneath Beijing, China. The adults and children of the city were forced to dig this war shelter themselves, mostly by hand.

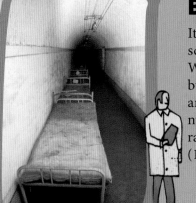

MOSCOW METRO 2

Underneath Moscow is a secret railway system built in the early to mid 20th century. The railway is supposedly larger than the real Moscow Metro (which is huge!). Tunnels reportedly run 25 km (15.5 mi.) out into the countryside to evacuate Soviet leaders in the case of war.

□ *The Russian government denied Metro 2 existed for many years. Explorers claim to have found their way in there in 1994.*

TAGANSKY

This huge command center — 7000 m² (75 000 sq. ft.) — is in a bunker 65 m (213 ft.) beneath central Moscow. Before it was declassified in 1995, it was kept fully equipped with food and water in case of nuclear attack.

□ *The Tagansky bunker was built to save VIPs if the Cold War became full war.*

CHEYENNE MOUNTAIN

Cheyenne Mountain Operations Center in Colorado is supposed to be secret, but has become famous. It was built in the 1960s, buried 600 m (2000 ft.) deep in a granite mountain. This is where the U.S. military spots and tracks any missiles fired across the world — and especially any that might be fired at the U.S. Entry is through a 1.5 km (1 mi.) long tunnel guarded by thick, blast-proof doors.

North American Aerospace Defense Command (NORAD) protects the skies above the United States and Canada from deep inside Cheyenne Mountain.

Every year on Christmas Eve, NORAD takes time off from its usual duties and tracks Santa Claus as he leaves the North Pole and delivers presents to children around the world.

WISH YOU WERE HERE?

Not all bunkers are dug close to big cities. In 1958, the U.S. government agreed to build a brand-new wing on the luxury Greenbrier Hotel in a quiet town in West Virginia. In exchange, they were also allowed to secretly build a huge bunker beneath the hotel. It was code-named "Project Greek Island" and could shelter 1100 government staff in case of a nuclear holocaust.

Right, a secret meeting room below the hotel.

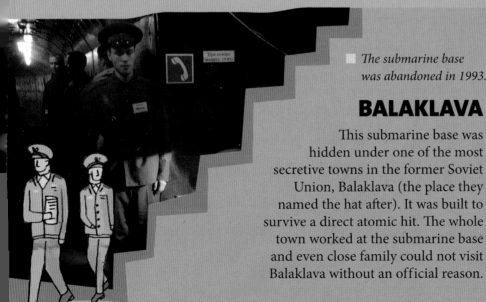

The submarine base was abandoned in 1993.

BALAKLAVA

This submarine base was hidden under one of the most secretive towns in the former Soviet Union, Balaklava (the place they named the hat after). It was built to survive a direct atomic hit. The whole town worked at the submarine base and even close family could not visit Balaklava without an official reason.

LIFE ON MARS?

If we run out of gold, oil and gems to mine on Earth, or we mess up the planet too much to grow food, could we move somewhere else and start digging there? Mars, for example?

If water once flowed here, was there life on Mars millions of years ago?

Mining machinery could be transported to Mars from Earth.

Precious minerals could be mined here and shipped back to Earth.

DESTINATION MARS?

What if we made such a mess of our own planet that we needed to find a home on another one? Or simply thought it would be really cool to go on an interplanetary adventure for our holidays? If life once existed on Mars — and it seems more and more likely that it did — perhaps this planet would be our best bet. But, frankly, with Mars's unfriendly atmosphere, it would be wise to build underground. Thankfully, new tunneling machines could make this possible. And scientists have already begun safeguarding our food supplies for the future.

Nobody needs to dig tunnels with spades anymore. Huge tunnel-boring machines with whirring steel cutters are able to munch right through rock.

NOT SO BORING

Engineers are working on tunneling machines that use heat and push forward instead of digging. In the future, nuclear-powered tunneling machines might melt their way through solid granite, instantly coating the wall of the tunnel in smooth glass. Whole cities could be built deep under the ground.

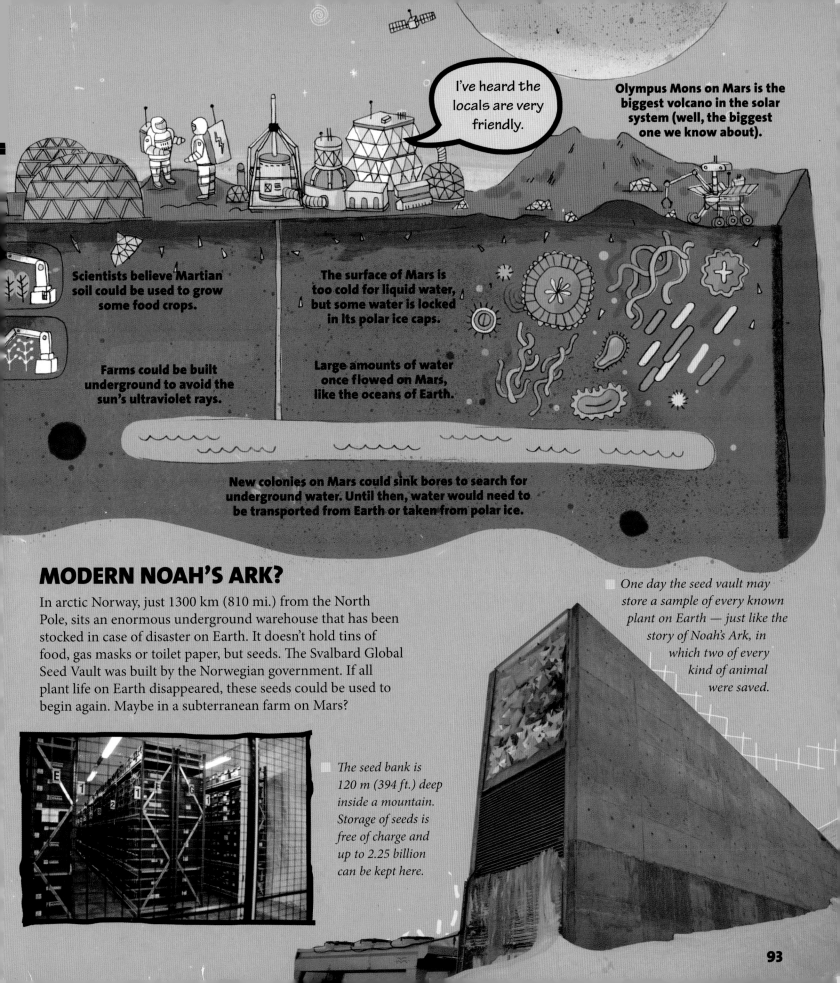

Olympus Mons on Mars is the biggest volcano in the solar system (well, the biggest one we know about).

I've heard the locals are very friendly.

Scientists believe Martian soil could be used to grow some food crops.

The surface of Mars is too cold for liquid water, but some water is locked in its polar ice caps.

Farms could be built underground to avoid the sun's ultraviolet rays.

Large amounts of water once flowed on Mars, like the oceans of Earth.

New colonies on Mars could sink bores to search for underground water. Until then, water would need to be transported from Earth or taken from polar ice.

MODERN NOAH'S ARK?

In arctic Norway, just 1300 km (810 mi.) from the North Pole, sits an enormous underground warehouse that has been stocked in case of disaster on Earth. It doesn't hold tins of food, gas masks or toilet paper, but seeds. The Svalbard Global Seed Vault was built by the Norwegian government. If all plant life on Earth disappeared, these seeds could be used to begin again. Maybe in a subterranean farm on Mars?

One day the seed vault may store a sample of every known plant on Earth — just like the story of Noah's Ark, in which two of every kind of animal were saved.

The seed bank is 120 m (394 ft.) deep inside a mountain. Storage of seeds is free of charge and up to 2.25 billion can be kept here.

INDEX

Credits and Acknowledgments

Key: tl=top left; tcl=top center left; tc=top center; tcr=top center right; tr=top right; cl=center left; c=center; cr=center right; bl=bottom left; bcl=bottom center left; bc=bottom center; bcr=bottom center right; br=bottom right; bg=background.

ALA=Alamy; **BAL**=Bridgeman Art Library; **CBT**=Corbis Traditional Licensing; **DT**=Dreamstime; **GI**=Getty Images; **iS**=iStockphoto.com; **SH**=Shutterstock; **TF**=Topfoto; **TPL**=photolibrary.com.

Photographs

8bc, cr **iS**; bl **SH**; 10bl **CBT**; br **iS**; tl, tr **SH**; 10–11c **iS**; 11bl, tl **iS**; 13cr **CBT**; c **iS**; cl **SH**; 16–17bc **ALA**; t **GI**; 17br **CBT**; 18tl **CBT**; br **GI**; bl, tr **TPL**; 19bl **GI**; c **SH**; tl **TPL**; 20c **GI**; 20–21c **GI**; 21br, cr **iS**; 22bl, br **ALA**; bc **CBT**; c **iS**; 24bl **CBT**; tl **TPL**; 25tc, tcr **CBT**; tcr **TPL**; 26c **GI**; 26–27bc, tl **BAL**; b **iS**; 27br **ALA**; tr **GI**; c **TPL**; 30c **ALA**; br, cr **GI**; 31c, cl **GI**; tl **SH**; 32–33bc **CBT**; bg, c **GI**; 33bc, cr, tc **CBT**; 34bc, tr **CBT**; bl, cr **iS**; 35br **GI**; cl **iS**; 36bc **GI**; 37bc **TPL**; 40cl, cr **CBT**; bc, tc **GI**; 41cr, tl **CBT**; 42cl **ALA**; bl **CBT**; bcr, tcr **GI**; tr **SH**; 42–43bg **iS**; 43bcl, bcr, tcl, tcr **GI**; 44bc, cr **CBT**; br, cl, tl **GI**; 45bl,

tr **CBT**; 46br **TF**; 46–47c **TF**; 47bc **ALA**; tc **CBT**; cr **TF**; 48bc, bcr, br **SH**; 48–49c **CBT**; bg **GI**; 49bc **ALA**; br, c, cr **CBT**; tc, tl **SH**; 52tr **GI**; bc, br, c, cr **SH**; 53bcr **CBT**; cl, tr **GI**; bc, tl **SH**; 54tr **ALA**; bc **CBT**; c **GI**; bl, cl, tcr **SH**; 54–55b **iS**; 55cl **ALA**; bc, tr **CBT**; bcr, bl, tcr **SH**; 56cr **CBT**; cl **GI**; bc **SH**; 56–57tc **GI**; bc **iS**; 57cr, tc **CBT**; c **GI**; bc **SH**; 58br, c, cr **CBT**; cl **SH**; 59cr **ALA**; cl **GI**; 62cl **ALA**; br **CBT**; cr, bl **GI**; 63cl, bc, tr, tc **GI**; 64c **ALA**; br, cr **CBT**; tl **SH**; 65c **GI**; 66bc **CBT**; tl, tr **SH**; 67bc **GI**; cl, tr **iS**; tl **SH**; 68tr **CBT**; bc **GI**; 72tr **CBT**; bl **iS**; 73tr **BAL**; br **CBT**; bl **TPL**; 74br, tl **GI**; cl **iS**; bc, cr **TPL**; 74–75c, c **TPL**; 75br **iS**; bl, tc **TPL**; 76bc **GI**; bl **SH**; 76–77bc **CBT**; 77br **GI**; tr **iS**; c **SH**; 80cl **CBT**; 80–81bc **CBT**; 81bc, cr **DT**; tl, tr **SH**; 82bl **CBT**; tc **SH**; 82–83bc, tc **GI**; 83 bc, bcr, tcr, tr **SH**; 84bl **SH**; 85bc, cl, cr **CBT**; tr **GI**; br **SH**; 88bl, cr **iS**; bc **SH**; 88–89c **SH**; 89br, c **iS**; bc, bl **SH**; 90tr **ALA**; bc **CBT**; c **GI**; tc, tl **SH**; 90–91c **ALA**; 91tc **CBT**; br **DT**; bl, cr **GI**; tr, tr **SH**; 93br **CBT**; bl **GI**.

Illustrations

All illustrations by James Gulliver Hancock/The Jacky Winter Group except 11c; 12b; tc, tl; 12–13tc; 31bl; 35tr; 72–73c; 92br © Weldon Owen Publishing.

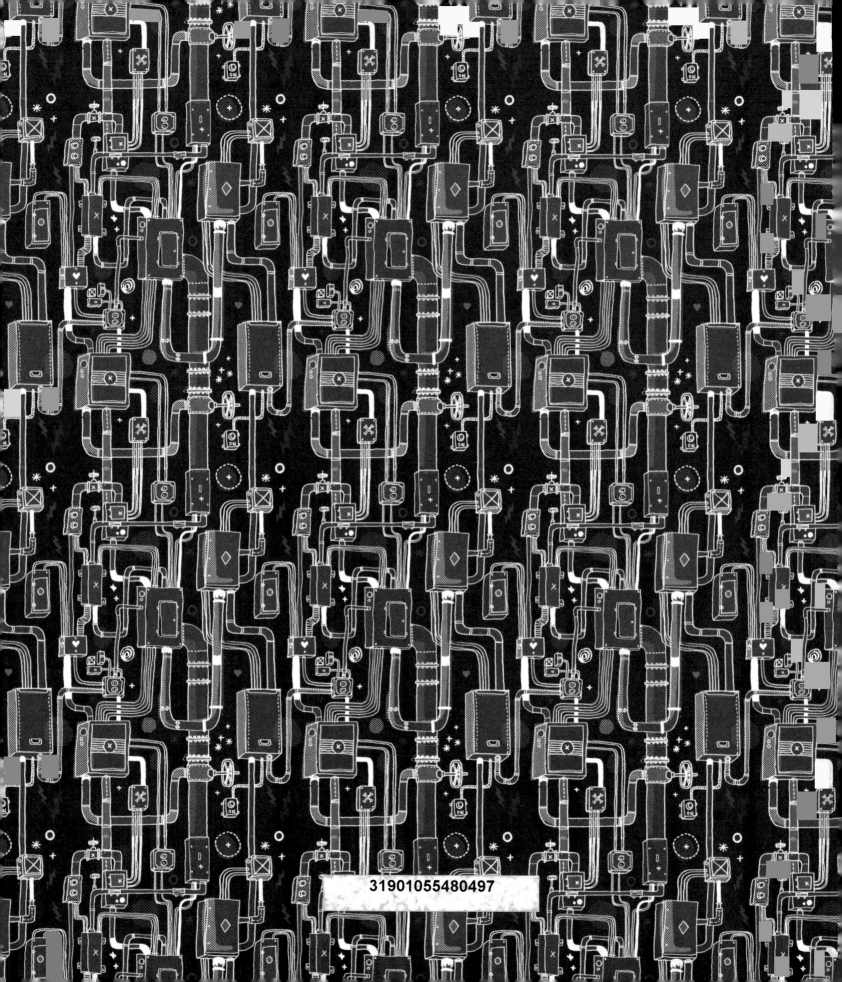

31901055480497